Also Available

Understanding PC Software

by
R. A. Penfold

BERNARD BABANI (publishing) LTD
THE GRAMPIANS
SHEPHERDS BUSH ROAD
LONDON W6 7NF
ENGLAND

Please Note

Although every care has been taken with the production of this book to ensure that any projects, designs, modifications and/or programs etc. contained herewith, operate in a correct and safe manner and also that any components specified are normally available in Great Britain, the Publishers and Author(s) do not accept responsibility in any way for the failure (including fault in design) of any project, design, modification or program to work correctly or to cause damage to any equipment that it may be connected to or used in conjunction with, or in respect of any other damage or injury that may be so caused, nor do the Publishers accept responsibility in any way for the failure to obtain specified components.

Notice is also given that if equipment that is still under warranty is modified in any way or used or connected with home-built equipment then that warranty may be void.

British Library Cataloguing in Publication Data
Penfold, R. A.
    Understanding PC software
    I. Title
    005.36

    ISBN 0 85934 248 4

Printed and Bound in Great Britain by Cox & Wyman Ltd, Reading

Preface

The IBM PCs and compatibles are now more or less the automatic choice for business computing applications, as well as some scientific, technical, and other applications. They are versatile computers which are backed-up by an unrivalled range of applications software and specialist hardware devices. Within reason, a PC can handle any application. Whether you require a system that can handle simple word processing, or one that can run complex scientific simulations, there is almost certainly a PC based system that fulfils your requirements. Furthermore, the popularity of the PCs means that they are manufactured in huge quantities, resulting in them being very competitively priced.

There is a problem for anyone who is new to computing in that there is a lot of terminology to contend with, plus totally new ways of handling tasks. This book is concerned with the software side of PC computing, and it assumes very little previous knowledge of computer software. It is assumed that you know something about the hardware side of things, and that you can get the computer up and running. If you are unfamiliar with the hardware aspect of PCs, this is covered in a separate book (*Understanding PC Specifications*, BP282). The range of PC software available can be, to say the least, a bit confusing. What is the difference between a database and a spreadsheet, and will either be of any real use to you? It would be very easy to spend hundreds of pounds on unsuitable software, and many people have done just that!

All the main types of business computer software are covered in this book. This means word processors, graphics programs such as CAD (computer aided drawing), illustration programs, and business graphics software, desktop publishing (d.t.p.), databases, and spreadsheets. In fact the basics of all the main categories of business software are covered, which should enable you to decide which types of programs are genuinely of practical use to you, and avoid wasting money on totally unsuitable programs.

R. A. Penfold

Trademark Acknowledgements

Contents

Chapter 1

WORD PROCESSING

Possibly the most frequently asked question by those who are new to word processing is "how is word processing different to using a typewriter?" With a lot of electronic typewriters now having some quite advanced features, the difference between the two is perhaps not quite as clear-cut as it once was. The main difference is that with a word processor you type in a complete document, edit it, and then print out the hard copy once it has been perfected. Corrections are easily made, since the documents are initially held in the computer's memory, and are in a form where they can be easily changed. If you should change your mind about something once a document has been printed out, it will probably not take long to correct it and print out a fresh copy. However, for word processing to be really efficient, it is necessary to catch most of the errors before producing the hard copy. In fact this is true of many types of computing.

With a typewriter any mistakes must be corrected on the hard copy using "Tipp-Ex" (or whatever), which is relatively slow and messy. Some electronic typewriters have a screen which shows the last few lines typed in, and do not print out each character as it is typed on the keyboard. This enables any minor typing errors to be corrected before they are produced on the hard copy, which in this respect makes them almost as convenient as word processors. They are not quite as good though, since any mistakes must be spotted fairly quickly, or they will be reproduced on the hard copy. With a word processor corrections can easily be made anywhere in a document, and at any time prior to printing it out.

A word processor has editing facilities that go well beyond this simple error correction facility though. You can go to any point in a document and add or delete some text. This editing may involve one word, or several thousand words. You can even copy blocks of text, or move them to new positions in the document. In fact you have complete freedom to chop and change the document in any way you wish. This contrasts with

1

typewriting, where even quite minor changes can necessitate retyping a page, or even retyping a complete document.

Although some early word processor programs were somewhat limited with respect to the maximum document size they could handle, this is not a problem with most modern programs. The majority of modern word processor programs for the PCs can handle massive documents. A chapter of a book some 10,000 to 20,000 words in length is well within the capabilities of these programs, and in some cases documents many times larger than this can be accommodated. In practice the limiting factor may be the speed of the program, which can greatly reduce on some facilities when very large documents are loaded into the program. Probably most users will never have any problems with documents of excessive size for the program and (or) the computer. This is something that I have not experienced with my current word processing setup.

Word Wrapping

For someone who is used to operating an ordinary typewriter, the most obvious difference when switching to a word processor is often the word processor's word wrap facility. When using a typewriter you must operate the carriage return before reaching the end of a line. This takes you to the beginning of the next line, and prevents you from typing beyond the margin limits, or even right off the edge of the paper. With a word processor the carriage returns are added automatically by the program each time the end of a line is reached. This does not operate on a very simple level with words being split between two lines. If an entire word will not fit onto a line, it is moved to the beginning of the next line. For those who are used to adding their own carriage returns this can take a bit of getting used to, but it is actually much quicker and more convenient than adding the carriage returns yourself. Of course, you can still add carriage returns manually if necessary. They must be added at the ends of paragraphs, and headings for example.

A normal typewriter produces unjustified text. In other words, the lines are not of identical lengths, giving a ragged right hand margin. Word processors can be set to do things in this way, or they can be set to automatically provide justified text. With justified text extra spaces are added into lines, where necessary, so that all full lines are the same length, and a neat right hand margin is obtained. The text in this book is an example of justified text.

An overwhelming advantage of word processors in many applications is that they enable documents to be stored on computer disks. Print-outs of standard documents can be made as and when required, and there is no difficulty in making a few minor alterations in order to customise these standard documents. In fact, as we shall see later, customising standard letters, etc., is a task that can be largely automated in many cases. Producing several hundred personalised letters can often be achieved in a few minutes, plus the time taken for the system to print out all the letters. A high speed printer is definitely desirable if you are going to undertake much word processing of this type!

While there are marked differences between a word processor and a typewriter, I suppose that there are some strong similarities. In particular, a word processor is controlled via a typewriter style ("QWERTY") keyboard, which is also used for entering text. This has the usual shift and letter keys, spacebar, number/ punctuation keys, tab key, etc. However, even here there are significant differences between a typewriter and a word processor. As it has so many more functions, a word processor requires more keys in order to give access to these functions. Most PC keyboards now have 102 keys, which is about twice the number on a basic typewriter keyboard. This is not purely academic, and anyone who is experienced at using a typewriter and wishes to change over to word processing will obviously have to spend some time getting accustomed to the word processor keyboard with all its extra keys.

In Control

Word processors tend to be regarded by many as up-market type-writers, and from the description of them that I have provided so far you could get the impression that this description is not that "wide of the mark". This is not really the case though, and word processor programs have facilities that go well beyond the editing features described previously. The exact facilities vary consider-ably from one word processor program to another. Also, what is essentially the same facility might actually be somewhat different in certain respects on two different word processors. The word processor facilities described here are those of Wordperfect 5.0 (and later versions). This is currently the most popular up-market word processor program for the PCs. Bear in mind that the features of other word processors will be at least slightly different to those of Wordperfect 5.0. Also keep in mind that the facilities offered by inexpensive word processor programs are likely to fall well short of those described here.

Obviously some means of accessing the various features of a word processor is required. The way in which this operates varies considerably from one program to another. With many programs, and not just word processors, there is a menu bar across the top of the screen, and this is just a series of words which give access to various pop-down menus. Typical header words in the menu bar would be something like "PRINT", "EDIT", "SEARCH", "FILES", etc.

The required heading is usually selected by pressing the appropriate two keys. For example, pressing "Alt" and "F" could be used to select the "FILES" menu. A list of commands (the menu) would then appear on the screen beneath the appropriate menu bar header word. In this example there would probably be options such as "SAVE" (to save a document to disk), "LOAD" (to load a document from disk), "QUIT" (to exit from the program), and so on. The desired command can be selected using the cursor keys to move some form of on-screen indicator to the appropriate word, or simply pressing one of the letter keys (e.g. "L" for "LOAD" or "S" for "SAVE") might select the desired option. This depends on the particular program in use, but most programs that make use of menus now seem to permit both these methods of selection.

Many programs that have pop-down menus (but by no means all text programs) permit selection using the mouse as a pointing device. A mouse may well be an ideal method of controlling many graphics programs, but it is often less than ideal for operation with text programs where both hands are usually needed to operate the keyboard. Some word processor users seem to like mouse control, but my advice would be to largely forget this method, and to use the keyboard as much as possible.

Wordperfect 5.0 does not have any provision for pop-down menus (although I believe that this feature is present in version 5.1 of the program). Instead it is controlled via the function keys. Even where a program has pop-down menus, it is normal for so-called keyboard short cuts to be included as well. Pop-down menus offer a very easy method of controlling a program, and enable relatively inexperienced users to make full use of a program. However, experienced users can find this method of control a bit cumbersome. Control via keyboard control codes offers a quicker method of operating a program for those who take the time to learn them. If you are likely to use a program a great deal, then it is probably well worthwhile taking the time to learn at least some of the codes for the commands that you will use a great deal.

In the case of Wordperfect the commands are accessed via the function keys of the PC keyboard. There are at least ten of these keys on a PC keyboard, and on the face of it this limits the program to just ten functions. Each function key can be used on its own, or it can be pressed simultaneously with the "Alt", "Shift", or control ("Ctrl") key. This increases the maximum number of functions to forty. In most cases each of these codes gives access to a menu, rather than directly calling up a feature. Some of these menus are short lists of options displayed along the bottom line of the screen, while others are full screen types offering a large range of options (Fig. 1.1).

In some cases an option gives access to further menus, which might in turn give access to further menus. This enables literally hundreds of commands to be accessed, but some of the more obscure ones might only be reached after a number of key presses. In order to make control of the program easier for beginners, the program is supplied complete with a template which can be fitted above or around the function keys (depending on the type of keyboard in use). This shows the basic functions of each key, and to a large extent compensates for the lack of pop-down menus.

Editing
Adding text is basically just a matter of placing the cursor where you want the new text to go, and then typing it in. The new text can be added at the beginning of any existing text, at the end, or anywhere in between. The program normally operates in the "insert" mode, which simply means that any existing text to the right of or beneath the cursor is shifted to make room for any

5

```
Setup: Colours/Fonts

Attribute              Font   Foreground  Background  Sample
Normal                 N      C           A           Sample
Blocked                N      B           H           
Underline              Y      C           A           Sample
Strikeout              N      C           B           
Bold                   N      B           A           Sample
Double Underline       N      F           B           
Redline                N      E           B           Sample
Shadow                 N      A           D           Sample
Italics                N      B           D           
Small Caps             N      E           D           Sample
Outline                N      F           D           
Subscript              N      G           D           
Superscript            N      H           D           
Fine Print             N      B           A           Sample
Small Print            N      C           G           
Large Print            N      D           A           Sample
Very Large Print       N      A           C           Sample
Extra Large Print      N      F           A           Sample
Bold & Underline       Y      B           A           Sample
Other Combinations     N      A           G           Sample

Switch to switch; Move to copy settings       Doc 1
```

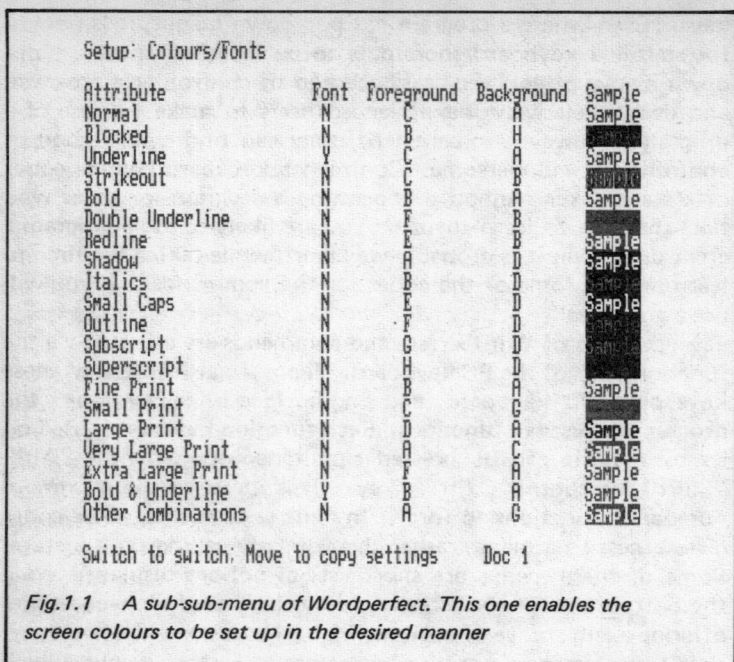

Fig.1.1   A sub-sub-menu of Wordperfect. This one enables the screen colours to be set up in the desired manner

new text that is added. The alternative mode is the "typeover" one, and in this mode any new text is added over (and effectively deletes) any existing text that gets in the way. This second mode is probably less useful, and should be used with care as it is easy to inadvertently type over some existing text.

Deleting text is easy, and pressing the "Del" key will delete the character above the cursor. The backspace key deletes the character to the left of the cursor. Deleting text one character at a time is very slow if a large amount of text is involved. Most keys have an automatic repeat facility if they are pressed continuously, but even with the aid of this facility it can take a long time to erase a large section of text. The quick way to erase a large section of text is to make use of the "block" function. This is not restricted to use when deleting text incidentally, and it can be used with many of the editing facilities. In fact some of the editing features are normally only operated in conjunction with the "block" facility.

In order to select a block of text you must first position the cursor at one end of the appropriate piece of text. The "block" command is then issued by pressing the "Alt" and F4 keys, after which the cursor is moved to the other end of the piece of text. The program will make it quite clear what text has been selected by showing it in inverse video on a monochrome system (i.e. black text on a light background), or in different foreground and background colours on a colour system. There are a number of manipulations that can be applied to a block of text, and one of the most simple is to delete it. In Wordperfect this is achieved simply by pressing the "Delete" key.

To be strictly accurate, there is slightly more to it than this. Having pressed the "Delete" key, the program will respond with a message along the bottom line of the screen asking if you are sure you wish to delete the block of text. It asks you to press the "Y" (for yes) key if you wish to delete the block of text, or the "N" (for no) key if you do not. Wordperfect will often ask you if you are sure that you wish to perform some major task before it actually goes ahead and does it. This is something that is common to many programs, especially where there is no "undo" facility. Some programs, especially graphics types, have a facility of this type which enables you to undo the last command if it was issued by mistake, or if it simply did not have the effect you expected. An undo command is by no means universal though, and seems to be relatively rare in text programs. It is sometimes conditional, and will not work with all commands.

By asking for confirmation before doing anything drastic to the document, the program largely avoids problems with severe damage to a document simply because the wrong key was pressed and the wrong command was accidentally issued. It does not guard against commands not having the desired effect though. Before issuing a command that could seriously damage a document it is advisable to save it to disk. If things should go badly wrong, you can then simply abandon the scrambled document, load in the intact version from the disk, and then try again. You can repeat this process as many times as is necessary.

Wordperfect does have a sort of undo command if text should be accidentally deleted. This is the "cancel" command in Wordperfect terminology, and it is called up by pressing the F1 key.

It is quite an advanced feature which enables you to toggle between the last two pieces of text to have been deleted, and one or both of them can be undeleted if desired. This feature only works on deleted text though, and it can not be used to reverse other commands.

Returning to the subject of block operations, Wordperfect has the usual copy and move commands. In both cases, having selected a block of text you position the cursor at the new position for the text, and then put it in place using the retrieve option. The move and copy commands differ in that with the move command the original block of text is deleted, whereas it is left intact by the copy command. A block of text can be copied as many times as you like incidentally, simply by repeatedly using the retrieve option.

With Wordperfect the copy and move instructions are not restricted to operating on a previously selected block of text. Instead, there are options for moving a word, sentence, or paragraph. The required word, sentence, or paragraph is selected simply by positioning the cursor within it prior to issuing the copy or move command. If a block of text is marked out before issuing one of these commands, then it will be assumed that this is the piece of text that must be manipulated, and the word, sentence, and paragraph options will not then be available. This is a very versatile system, but in my experience it is almost invariably the block option that is needed when using these commands.

Formatting

Word processing is not limited to simply typing in a document, doing any necessary editing, and then printing it out as one long and unvarying column of text. There are a number of formatting commands which give considerable control over how the finished document will look. At a fairly basic level, the "centre" command enables a line of text to be centred. When this command is issued the cursor goes to the middle of the current line. As text is typed in, it grows outwards from the middle of the line, and always remains nicely centred on the line. This facility is mainly used for headings, or possibly for sub-headings. However, it can be used for the main body of the text if desired, and it is not restricted to single lines. If some existing text must be centred, it is just a matter of selecting the text using a "block" instruction, and then issuing the "centre" instruction.

The underline facility is another simple formatting instruction, and it merely produces text that is underlined. Once again, this is a feature that is mainly used for headings and subheadings, but it can also be in the main body of the text if desired. Wordperfect actually enables a wide range of text styles (bold, italic, etc.) to be used if desired, and it can also accommodate a range of text sizes. A large range of fonts (character shapes) are also available. However, you need to keep in mind that your printer might not be able to handle large numbers of text styles, fonts, and sizes. Most printers can handle at least a few variations which can be used to enhance the appearance of documents. The main exceptions are daisy-wheel printers which require the daisy-wheel to be changed in order to change to a new text size, font, or style. This makes changes of font, etc., within a document a bit impractical.

An interesting feature of Wordperfect is its "columns" command. This can be used as an aid to producing lists and tables, or it can be used to put the text into what are generally termed "newspaper" style columns. In other words, the text runs down column one, continues down column two, then column three, and so on. Wordperfect gives considerable control over the column widths, spacing, etc., and the number of columns used. Up to twenty-four columns can be accommodated, although with most printers and paper sizes the practical maximum is likely to be just three or four columns.

Some word processors have a full WYSIWYG (what you see is what you get) display, and even show a reasonable representation of different text styles, sizes and fonts. Wordperfect does not do this on the normal display which is used when entering text, editing, and so on. This may seem rather crude in comparison to some other word processor programs, but it does mean that the display updates very fast, and this helps to give Wordperfect its generally high operating speed. If you type some text into the middle of a long document for example, there is no risk of you entering the text faster than Wordperfect can digest it. This is not true of all the word processors I have used, especially some of the full WYSIWYG types.

Very often it is not necessary to check the appearance of a page before it is printed out. Many documents are too simple to make this necessary, while with others you will know from experience that everything is the way you want it. Where it is necessary to check that the layout of the page is correct before printing it, the preview facility can be used to show an accurate representation of each page on the display. This is an option of the print command, and the program effectively prints to the screen rather than to the printer.

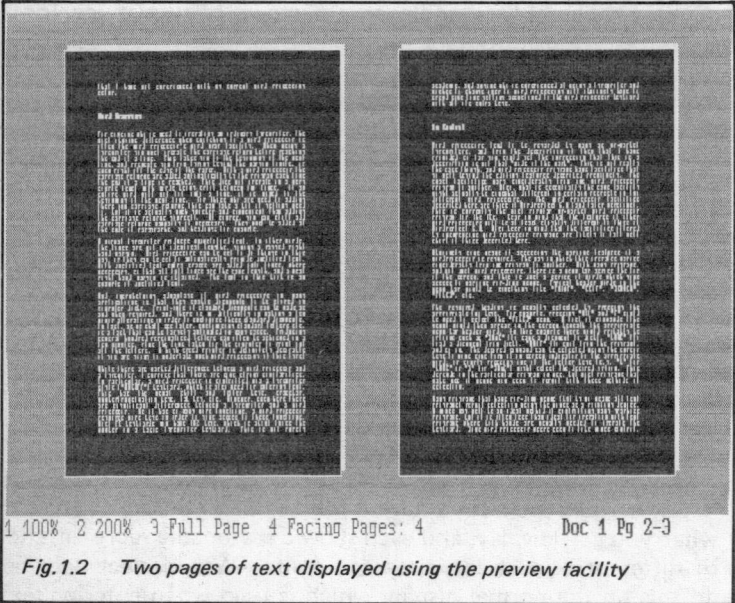

Fig.1.2   Two pages of text displayed using the preview facility

A problem with any WYSIWYG screen display is that the screen resolution will often be very much lower than that of the printer in use. Showing a full page or two facing pages on the screen will not usually give a very accurate representation. As can be seen from the screen dump of Figure 1.2, you do get a good overall impression of what the printed out pages will look like, and this is often all that is needed. Having a high resolution screen is a definite advantage as it gives a more accurate impression of the pages, and true WYSIWYG screens are normally only possible if the computer has some form of graphics display. Even with a relatively low resolution display, the preview screen should give a reasonable overall impression of what the printed out pages will look like. A zoom facility enables a small area of each page to be displayed over the full screen area (Fig. 1.3) so that it can be examined in detail. It is possible to scroll around a page so that the whole page can be viewed in detail, section by section.

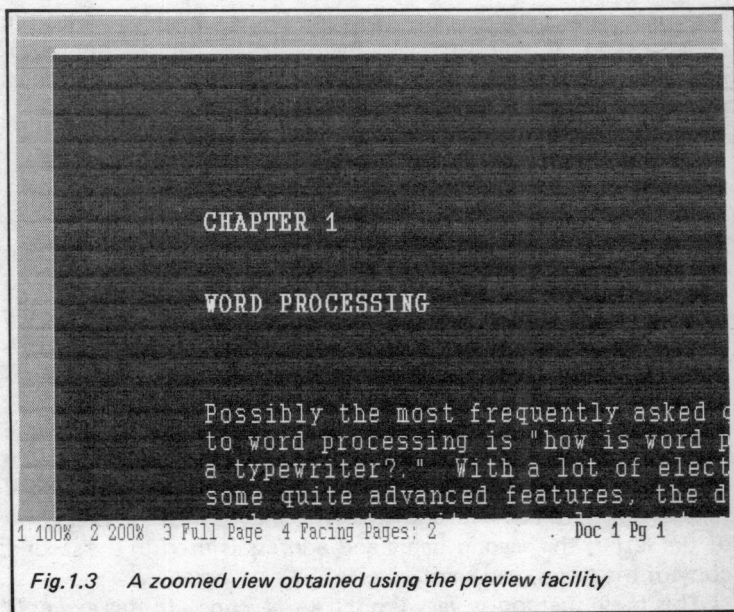

```
        CHAPTER 1


        WORD PROCESSING



        Possibly the most frequently asked q
        to word processing is "how is word p
        a typewriter?."  With a lot of elect
        some quite advanced features, the d
1 100%  2 200%  3 Full Page  4 Facing Pages: 2          . Doc 1 Pg 1
```

Fig.1.3   A zoomed view obtained using the preview facility

Mail Merge

One of the main attractions of word processors for many business users is the ease with which standard letters can be handled, particularly where it is necessary to send out the same letter to a large number of people. Obviously a standard letter can be done on the basis of starting "Dear Sir/Madam", "Dear Customer", or something of this type, instead of having the name of each person. Also, the address of the recipient can be omitted.

11

However, it is definitely preferable to have the letters personalised by including both the name and the address of the recipient on each one. They can be further personalised by including the name in the main text of the letter (something which tends to be done to excess in the circulars sent out by some mail order companies!).

One way of doing this would be to have someone go through each standard letter and manually add the personal touch to each one. This would not take long with a few letters, but is not very practical if dozens or more letters are involved. Virtually all word processors have a "mail merge" feature which enables the personalising of standard documents to be carried out automatically. The way in which this operates tends to vary considerably from one word processor program to another, but the aim is very much the same in each case.

Wordperfect handles mail merging by having two disk files. The first of these (the primary file) is the one which contains the standard document which must be personalised, while the second one (the secondary file) contains the list of names and addresses (or whatever). The second file is not just a simple list of names and addresses. The mail merge facility needs some way of knowing where to place items from the secondary file in the primary file. This is done by using special merge commands in both files. At the most basic level this is done by using merge codes to divide the secondary file into separate records. In other words, a merge code is used between each name and address in order to divide them into separate pieces of data which the program can work through. The first name and address is placed into the first copy of the letter, the second name and address is used in the second copy of the letter, and so on.

This basic method is very limited in its scope. In this example there is an obvious problem in that each name and address should ideally be separate pieces of data. They can then be used at different positions in the standard letter, rather than having to be used at the same place as a single entity. Wordperfect allows for this by enabling each record to be divided into numbered subsections if the appropriate merge codes are used. These subsections are called fields, and a large number of fields can be used if desired. For most purposes two or three will probably suffice though.

Obviously some means of indicating the positions of the various fields in the primary file is needed, and this is achieved by inserting the appropriate merge codes into the file. These merge codes use the field numbers so that you can call up whatever fields are needed and place them at any desired position in the primary file. The fields do not have to be used in sequence, and it is quite alright to use fields more than once or to leave some of them unused.

Once suitable primary and secondary files have been produced, it is just a matter of invoking the mail merge command, supplying the primary and secondary filenames, and then waiting while the program generates the letters. The letters will be generated in the form of a huge document stored in the computer's memory. This can be viewed on the screen, edited if desired, and printed out in the usual way.

This is obviously a very powerful feature which can be used in a variety of applications. I have only described the basic function of the mail merge facility, and the way it is used, but there are actually some additional mail merge commands which increase its versatility. Where any kind of customised document is required, the mail merge facility is likely to provide a means of producing good quality results with a minimum of effort. As with many types of computing, the initial setting up might be quite time-consuming. In this case it is the production of a suitable secondary file or files that is likely to be time-consuming. However, some time spent setting up the system and learning to use it is likely to be repaid many times over in the lifetime of the computer system.

A useful feature of many word processors, including Wordperfect, is their ability to read the PC's clock/calendar circuit and use this to place the correct date in documents. In its most simple form, all the program does is to place the date in the document in the form of ordinary text. A more advanced form of the date command puts a date code into the document. There is an important difference between the date text and the date code versions of this command. With the date text method, the date is always the same, and is the date when the document was created. If the document is called up at some later time, the date shown will be the original one. This is the date command that is used for most letters, where you may need to refer back to the letter to determine when it was sent.

With the date code method the date will always be the current one. This is mainly intended for standard letters that will be stored on disk, called up as and when necessary, personalised, printed out, and posted. Obviously the date shown on a standard letter should be the current one, and not the date when the letter was originally produced.

Graphics

Graphics is a term that is frequently encountered in computing, and it simply refers to any form of drawing, chart, or anything which does not consist purely of text. Until relatively recently most word processors lived up to their names, and could only handle text. This has now changed, and many word processors (including Wordperfect version 5.0 and later versions) have the ability to include graphics in documents.

It has to be stressed that Wordperfect, in common with other word processors, does not in itself have the ability to generate graphics. It does have some basic line drawing commands, but these are only intended for use in such things as lists, tables, and very basic charts. Any graphics that are required have to be drawn up and perfected using a separate program, or possibly even several programs if totally different types of drawing are required. The subject of graphics programs will not be pursued further here since it is a subject that is covered in some detail in Chapter 2.

It is only fair to point out that while Wordperfect can import graphics from a wide range of programs, it can not accommodate the file formats of all drawing programs. Some word processors that have a graphics facility are somewhat less accommodating in the range of formats that they support. The Wordperfect manual lists the graphics formats that are supported. The range of programs that can produce compatible graphics files is actually quite a lot larger than this list would suggest. One reason for this is that many graphics programs can produce files in their own format, and in one or more other formats. Therefore, a program which can produce files in one of the formats mentioned in the manual should be able to produce files that can be loaded into Wordperfect.

Another reason is that there are some file formats which are not specific to one particular program, and which can be produced by numerous graphics programs. Probably the best example of this is the HPGL (Hewlett Packard Graphics Language) format. This was originally intended as a means of sending drawings from graphics programs to a pen plotter. A pen plotter is simply a mechanical device which produces drawings, charts, etc., under computer control, and draws them on paper using a pen. A sort of mechanical draughtsman in fact! Although the HPGL language was originally conceived as a means of sending graphics to a plotter, it is now used as a means of swapping drawings between programs, and is one of the best means of achieving this type of transfer.

A third reason for many drawing programs being compatible with Wordperfect is that graphics format conversion programs are available. In fact simple programs of this type are often included with graphics programs, and a conversion utility is included as part of the Wordperfect package. Some of the graphics programs that Wordperfect supports must have their files processed by this or a similar conversion utility before they can be loaded into Wordperfect documents.

It is only fair to point out that graphics format conversion programs are not always 100% effective. To be honest about it, there is always a risk of things going slightly wrong when a graphics file produced by one program is loaded into another program. Using a conversion utility simply increases the risk of things going amiss by adding an extra stage in the process. Where possible, with this type of thing it is always best to test the compatibility of programs with a few test drawings before going ahead and buying anything. In most cases there will be no problems, or only some minor ones that can be overcome or simply put up with, but occasionally there can be a serious incompatibility problem for no obvious reason, and possibly no solution to the problem.

If suitable graphics files can be produced, then loading them into Wordperfect is fairly straightforward. I find that with Wordperfect it is generally easier if all the text is entered first, and then the graphics are introduced into the text at suitable positions. The first task when importing a drawing into a program is to produce a graphics box of the required size. This box can actually have its border indicated by a line, or it can be a reserved area of the page with no border marking. Once a graphics box has been produced, the appropriate drawing can be loaded into it.

There are various options associated with captions for the drawing, and in my experience it is better to caption graphics using Wordperfect's facilities, rather than importing graphics complete with captions. One of the most common problems when transferring graphics from one program to another is that of the text width changing. For some reason this usually seems to manifest itself in the form of "stretched" text which no longer fits into the space allocated to it. Probably the opposite problem of "compressed" text is equally common, but is usually overlooked. If the text takes up less space than it was allocated, it may not matter. If it goes outside its intended borders it is almost certain to produce unacceptable results.

Wordperfect provides some simple graphics editing facilities, but these are pretty basic. This is all one could reasonably expect from a word processor, and as pointed out previously, each drawing must be produced and perfected in a separate program, and then loaded into Wordperfect as "fait accompli". The editing commands only permit global changes to be made to the drawing, such as rotating it in 90 degree steps or changing its size relative to the graphics box.

When using the normal editing screen, any graphics in a document will not be visible. Their positions are marked, but if you want to check that the pages look the way you want, the preview facility must be used. It is perhaps worthwhile mentioning that Wordperfect is supplied with some clip-art, which is simply a collection of predrawn images which can be used in documents. Further clip-art can be purchased, and this offers a useful (but in some respects limited) alternative to using a graphics program to produce your own artwork.

Spelling Checker
At one time spelling checkers were mainly in the form of separate programs which could be used to check the contents of files produced using a word processor. These days most word processors, apart from those at the low cost end of the market, have

fully integrated spelling checker facilities. The spelling checker may still be what is virtually a separate program, but to anyone using the word processor it appears to be just another one of the available commands. Wordperfect is equipped with an excellent spelling checker facility.

For anyone who is going to use a spelling checker it is important to understand the basic way in which they function. What a spelling checker actually does is to compare each word in the document against a large dictionary of words stored on disk. If a word is not found in the dictionary, then it is assumed to be a likely spelling error and is pointed out to the user. It might be a genuine spelling error, but there is also the possibility that it is a correctly spelled word which does not happen to be in the spelling checker's dictionary.

Many of the early spelling checkers had very limited vocabularies of around 20,000 words or so, which rendered them of little practical value. Although 20,000 words may seem to be a reasonable vocabulary, it should be remembered that all the variations on each word must be included as separate entries in the dictionary. For example, simply having the word "include" is not adequate. It would also be necessary to have variations such as includes, included, and including. Wordperfect has a dictionary of about 110,000 words, which includes the standard variations on the basic words, and a large number of the more obscure words in circulation. This ensures that it does not keep pointing out spelling mistakes that are actually perfectly valid words which do not happen to be included in the program's dictionary.

In common with virtually all other spelling checker facilities, the one in Wordperfect permits the user to add to the dictionary. The types of thing that usually need to be added are frequently used place names, abbreviations, technical terms, and pieces of jargon. These can be added to the dictionary as and when the spelling checker turns them up, and over a period of time the number of spelling mistakes erroneously picked out by the checker should greatly reduce.

In use you have the option of checking an entire document, just one page, or even just a single word. There is also a "look up" facility which enables you to enter words from the keyboard which are then checked.

The spelling checker has an "alternatives" feature which greatly streamlines the correction of spellings. If a suspected spelling mistake is found, the program will look through its dictionary for words that are similar to the one in question. Apart from looking at words which have similar letter patterns, it will also consider things phonetically. In other words, it will look at words which sound similar to the suspect word, even if the spellings are substantially different. As a simple example, entering the word "phish" results in the spelling checker offering these alternatives:—

A.   face
B.   fiche
C.   fish

If the spelling checker offers the correct spelling, it can be entered into the document merely by pressing the appropriate letter key (e.g. in the example above, pressing the "C" key would result in "phish" being changed to "fish"). You have the alternatives of skipping over the word, manually editing it, or adding it to the dictionary.

Most spelling checkers have a double word occurrence detection facility, and Wordperfect is no exception. A double word occurrence is where a word appears twice in succession, as in this example:—

The quick brown fox jumped over the the lazy dog.

This may not seem to be a particularly useful feature, but double word occurrences are a common form of mistake, and they are not as easy to spot as you might think. They are particularly easy to miss if the first occurrence is at the end of a line, and the second occurrence is at the beginning of the next line.

The spelling checker includes a word count facility. Some word processors keep a running count of the number of words in a document, and display it somewhere on the screen. However, most only provide a word count if they are requested to, and apparently there are still a few word processors which do not include this feature at all. A word count facility is probably not that useful for general office applications, but it is essential to many word processor users who produce long documents (such as computer books).

A good spelling checker is a very useful feature indeed, even if you are good at spelling. No one knows how to spell every word, and typing errors are easily made. A spelling checker can help you to produce much more professional results when producing practically any type of document.

Thesaurus

A thesaurus, or a synonym finder, is a feature that is generally only found in the more up-market word processor programs, such as Wordperfect. When producing long documents you can often find that a few words keep cropping up time and time again. Sometimes these may be technical terms or names. In such cases there will probably be no alternative but to keep on using these words, phrasing things to avoid any unnecessary usage of them. In most cases though, there will be alternatives to the over-used words, and the Wordperfect thesaurus can be used to find suitable alternatives.

One way of using the thesaurus is to first place the cursor within the word for which alternatives are required. If the thesaurus command is then issued, the program goes into a split screen mode (Fig. 1.4), and any synonyms for the word in question will be displayed in the lower section of the screen (possibly with an antonym being provided as well). The upper part of the screen displays part of the document being edited. An alternative method is to invoke the command with the cursor not positioned within a word. You can then type in a word once the command has executed and the program has gone into the split screen mode. Even using the first method of invoking this command, you still have the option of looking up alternatives for words typed into the keyboard.

Obviously the program can not find alternatives for every word. In some cases words simply do not have any real alternatives. In other cases words might not be included in the vocabulary of the thesaurus. However, it can usually come up with at least a few suggestions. It will sometimes manage some alternatives for words for which you might expect to defeat it. For example, the word "red" is one that does not seem to be a very promising prospect, but Wordperfect provides these alternatives:

```
(possibly with an antonym being provided as well). The upper
part of the screen displays part of the document being edited.
An alternative method is to invoke the command with the cursor
not positioned within a word. You can then type in a word once

┌command=(n)══════════════╤command=(v)═════════════╤command=(ant)═════════════
│ 1 A ·authority          │                        │ 7  · incompetence
│   B ·control            │ 4   ·control           │
│   C ·dominion           │     ·govern            │
│   D ·leadership         │     ·rule              │ 8  ·follow
│   E ·rule               │     ·supervise         │    ·obey
│                         │                        │
│ 2 F ·charge             │ 5   ·adjure            │
│   G ·directive          │     ·charge            │
│   H  injunction         │     ·dictate           │
│   I ·order              │     ·instruct          │
│                         │     ·order             │
│ 3 J ·ability            │                        │
│   K ·comprehension      │ 6   ·demand            │
│   L ·expertise          │     ·exact             │
│   M ·mastery            │     ·impel             │
│   N ·skill              │     ·require           │

1 Replace Word; 2 View Doc; 3 Look Up Word; 4 Clear Column; 0
```

*Fig.1.4   Some Wordperfect commands, including the thesaurus
command, use a split screen*

```
  *A.    cardinal
   B.    crimson
   C.    maroon
   D.    ruby
   E.    scarlet
   F.    vermilion
```

Some of the suggested words are usually marked with a " * ",
and this indicates that by pressing the appropriate letter key the
program can be made to provide synonyms of this synonym. For
instance, in the example given here, pressing the "A" key would
provide some synonyms of the word cardinal.

A thesaurus command can be of great help to those who
produce long documents, but it needs to be used carefully.
Many words have more than one meaning, and to help avoid
confusion Wordperfect puts the synonyms into groups, with

each group representing alternatives for a different meaning of the word in question. You obviously need to be careful to select a synonym that covers the correct meaning of the word. Also, bear in mind that some of the suggestions are likely to be accurate alternatives, while others may not be particularly suitable in the particular context in which you are using the word. This may all become abundantly clear if you look up synonyms of a synonym, then a synonym of that synonym, and so on. If you are not careful you can soon end up with lists of words which bear no obvious relationship at all to the word that you looked up originally. Some thought needs to be given when selecting alternatives, and unfamiliar words are probably best avoided, just in case they are not really appropriate in the context in which you are using the word.

Finally

This by no means covers all the features of Wordperfect and similar up-market word processor programs. There are numerous minor but useful features. As a few examples of these, there are the "search" and "replace" facilities. The search facility merely looks through a document for a specified string of characters. The replace facility takes things a step further, and having found the specified string of characters, it is replaced with another user supplied string. A typical use of this feature would be where you find you have been using the wrong spelling for a word. The search facility can find the incorrectly spelt word, and the replace facility can be used to change it to the correct spelling.

The sort command is another useful feature. This is mainly used to sort lists into alphabetical order. As an example of this, the index for this book was produced in no particular order, with the sort facility of Wordperfect then placing it into the correct alphabetical order.

Many word processors have the ability to handle more than one document at a time. This is sometimes done using split screen and "window" techniques, so that more than one document at a time can be displayed. Alternatively, you can switch from one document to another, with only one or the other being shown on the screen at any one time (which is the normal method for Wordperfect). Some word processors can handle several documents at once, and this is a facility which is intended more for programmers than for normal business purposes. With Wordperfect only two documents at a time can be handled, which is all that is normally needed.

The basic idea is that if a large document is being produced, and you suddenly need to produce one or two quick letters or memos, you can switch to the second document mode and produce the letters or memos. You can then switch back to the main document and carry straight on where you left off. Another use is where you are producing one document, and you need to keep referring to another one. With both documents loaded into the word processor, you can quickly switch backwards and forwards between them, as necessary.

One of the most powerful features of Wordperfect is its macro facility. This enables a series of commands to be stored on disk, and called up by pressing as few as two keys ("Alt" plus one of the letter keys). This may not seem to be particularly useful, but when using a word processor you can find that you frequently go through the same sequence of commands. A typical example would be where documents are printed in two or three standard formats, and before printing out a document you have to go through the appropriate set of formatting commands. A lot of time can be saved by using two or three macros to store the sets of formatting commands. The Wordperfect macro facility actually goes somewhat beyond this basic scheme of things. It has some facilities which are similar to those of a programming language. This enables practically anything (within reason) to be achieved using a macro, but it can take some time and a lot of ingenuity to perfect complex macros.

Although it has not been possible to include all the features of Wordperfect here, the major ones have been covered, and this should give you a good idea of the capabilities of a modern word processor. They are certainly more than just up-market typewriters!

Chapter 2

GRAPHICS

If you need to produce technical illustrations, sketches, business charts, diagrams, etc., there are a wide range of drawing programs available which can handle these tasks. These programs all come under the general heading of "graphics", but there are a number of totally different types of program in this category. It is important to realise that graphics programs are almost invariably designed for use in the production of a particular type of drawing. They may be usable for generating other types of drawing, but would almost certainly be very slow and limited when used to produce drawings outside their normal sphere of operation. In some cases these programs are strictly for one type of drawing, and are of no use at all for anything else. Clearly it is essential to choose graphics software which accurately matches your application. If you must produce several different types of drawing, then you may well need two or more graphics programs in order to produce them all efficiently.

Pixel Graphics

Drawing programs come in two basic forms — the vector and pixel based types. The pixel oriented programs are normally called "paint" programs. The vector based programs are mostly of the CAD (computer aided drafting or computer aided drawing) and illustration types.

Pixel based programs are the more simple type, and they work at the screen resolution. This is an important factor, since it places very definite limits on the resolution that can be obtained, and therefore limits the quality of the final output. This limitation on the quality of the final output can make pixel graphics unsuitable for some applications, but it may not matter in others. This really depends on the resolution obtained, and the type of graphics you will be producing. If you have a PC with a CGA colour screen operating at 320 by 200 pixels, this is unlikely to give a good quality final printout unless the drawing is reproduced quite small.

Maximum output quality is obtained with a one-to-one relationship between the screen pixels and the dots of the output device. Using an output device capable of 300 dots per inch resolution, this would give optimum quality with the drawing just over an inch wide by 0.66 inches high! Higher screen resolutions give greater scope, and with an 800 by 600 pixel super V.G.A. screen at 300 dots per inch, the optimum size for the final output would be a more useful 2.66 inches by 2 inches.

It is not strictly accurate to say that drawings are limited to the same resolution as the display screen. It is possible to have a drawing that (in pixel terms) is larger than the screen, with the screen only showing part of it at any one time. Some paint programs do offer this over-size screen facility, but it is by no means a universal feature. In practice the amount of memory available usually limits the drawing size to something not that much larger than the screen size. With some paint programs part of the screen is taken up by menu bars, etc., effectively reducing the screen size. This does not normally reduce the drawing resolution very much though.

Paint programs are normally used for simple sketch type illustrations, although many can handle quite impressive looking multi-coloured "paintings" if that is what you need. They are not suitable for most technical illustrations, diagrams, etc., because their resolution is simply not adequate to carry all the necessary detail. Any graphics program is likely to take a certain amount of time and effort to master, but paint programs are probably the easiest type to learn. Much work with paint programs is done by simply drawing on the screen free-hand using the mouse to control the on-screen "pen". Drawing free-hand using a mouse is not quite as easy as you might think, and this aspect of paint programs can take some time to master. All paint programs seem to have good editing facilities so that it is reasonably easy to correct any mistakes you make.

Most paint programs can be made to operate with a digitising tablet, and it is then possible to use a pen-type drawing instrument instead of the puck (the digitising equivalent of a mouse). Even if the paint program has no support for a digitising tablet, many of these devices come complete with mouse emulation software. This enables them to be used with any program that has mouse support, which includes all the paint programs I have encountered. The tablet will probably operate in relative mode (like a mouse) rather than in absolute mode (which is the normal mode for digitising tablets). However, for a paint program either mode is perfectly suitable.

There is a definite advantage in using a pen-type tool for free-hand drawing. It is the type of tool we have all used for drawing since we were toddlers, giving it an intuitive quality that is lacking when using a mouse-type pointing device. Even so, it can still take a while to become completely accustomed to using one of these implements. It takes a while to get acclimatised to drawing on the digitising tablet with the results appearing on the screen of the monitor. It is perhaps worth pointing out that any drawing program can be difficult to use at first, simply because it involves a totally alien way of doing things. Most people soon get used to computerised methods of drawing though, and use graphics programs to full effect.

With most paint programs there are many drawing facilities in addition to simple free-hand drawing. Special commands for drawing arcs, circles, polygons, etc., are normally included. There are usually options that permit enclosed areas to be filled with blocks of colours or even complex patterns. Text in various sizes and fonts can normally be added, and there may even be things such as various nib shapes that permit calligraphic effects to be obtained, and a "spray paint" facility that gives an effect much like painting using an aerosol spray can.

Deluxe Paint II Enhanced is an example of a popular paint program for the PCs. The screen dump of Figure 2.1 shows the Deluxe Paint II Enhanced (hereafter referred to as just "DP2") screen layout, complete with a piece of on-screen artwork. Like many modern programs, DP2 makes use of a menu bar across the top of the screen, with pop-down menus being used to select the required command under the selected heading. To obtain a menu you simply use the mouse to move the on-screen pointer over the appropriate menu heading, and then press the left mouse button. The menu then pops down beneath the heading word. The required command is obtained by moving the pointer down the menu to the appropriate word and then releasing the right-hand mouse button. You are in no doubt as to which word you have selected, since it is shown in inverse video (i.e. white letters on a black background instead of the usual black letters

Fig. 2.1   The Deluxe Paint II Enhanced screen layout, with a cartoon being drawn up

on a white background).

These pop-down menus often lead to further menus or control panels. Figure 2.2 for example, shows "Delete" sub-menu, while Figure 2.3 shows the control panel which is used to set the colours in the pallet (i.e. the colours that are available for you to draw with). In this case the program is operating in the VGA 640 × 480 pixel mode, which offers a pallet around a quarter of a million colours, but with no more than sixteen different colours on the screen at once. Slider controls operated using the mouse and an on-screen pointer enable the required colours to be mixed quite easily and quickly.

Incidentally, many programs now use this method of menu control, but possibly with some slight differences in the exact way in which the system operates. With many programs, for example, pressing the mouse button results in the menu dropping

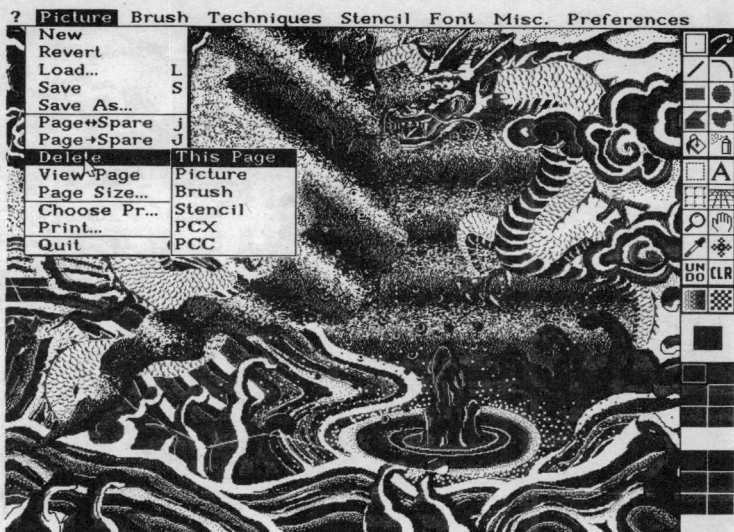

Fig. 2.2   This screen dump shows the "Picture" menu, and the "Delete" sub-menu. Note the use of inverse video to indicate the selected function

down. It then stays in place when the mouse button is released. A further "click" of the mouse button is used to select the desired menu option.

The menu bar and pop-down menus are mainly used for commands that will not be selected very frequently. This includes commands such as saving and loading artwork to and from disk, changing the text size, and the various special effects that are available.   The main drawing commands are selected using the icons down the right-hand side of the screen. An icon is simply a small on-screen drawing which graphically represents an available function. As a couple of examples, the straight line (second from the top in the left-hand column) is used when you wish to draw straight lines, and the spray-can (fifth from the top in the right-hand column) is used to select the spray-can effect. Other features available using the icons include arcs, text, undoing

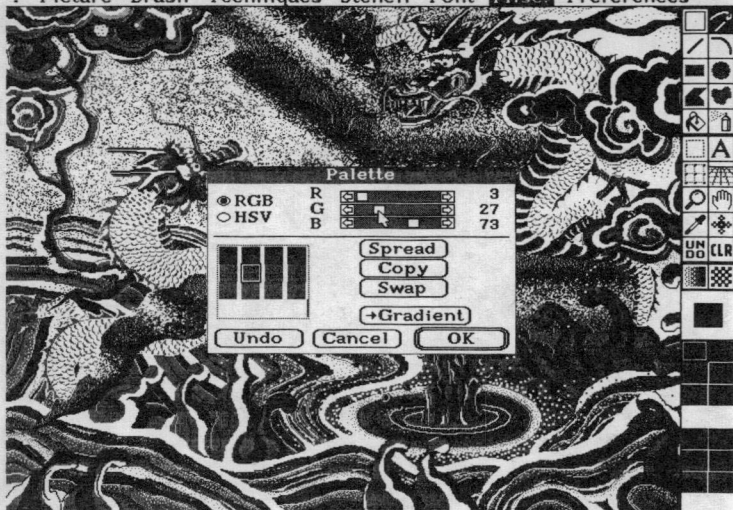

Fig. 2.3   The palette control panel. Colours are adjusted using the three on-screen slider controls

the last drawing operation, circles/ellipses, filled shapes of three types, and the ability to fill enclosed areas with the required colour or pattern. Figure 2.4 shows examples of several basic types of drawing element, including the spray-can effect, filled shapes, and different text styles/sizes.

The magnifying glass icon gives access to the zoom feature, which gives a form of split screen operation. The right-hand side of the screen shows a small area of the screen much larger than normal, and several degrees of magnification are available. The left-hand section shows the same area of the screen, but at normal size. Figure 2.5 shows the zoom feature in operation. The point of this is that it makes it easy to make fine adjustments to the drawing. Even with a very high resolution screen having minute pixels, if a high zoom level is used, the pixels are large and easily edited in the zoomed view. This is sometimes termed "fat bit" editing.

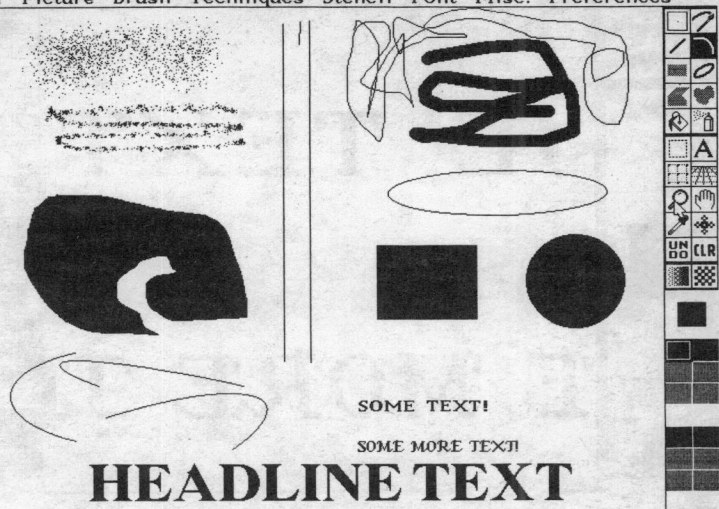

HEADLINE TEXT

Fig. 2.4 Some of DP2's basic drawing elements. The top left-hand corner shows the spray-can effect

The more up-market paint programs (including DP2) have some quite sophisticated features such as three dimensional effects, and are very capable if you are able to fully master them. I suppose that this is the major drawback of paint programs. If you have some artistic talent, it is not too difficult to learn to use a paint program effectively, and to produce the artwork that you require. On the other hand, if your artistic talents are strictly limited, you may be able to learn to use the program's facilities, but you may never produce anything more than doodles which are no use for the final product.

Another point to bear in mind if you intend to produce your own artwork using a paint program is that it can be much more time-consuming than you might expect. It is surprising how fast time passes when you are using one of these programs, even once you have become accustomed to using the program. Producing

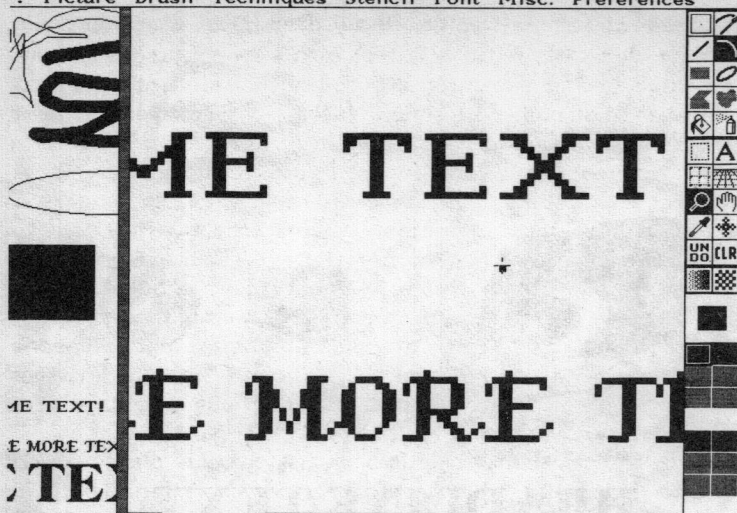

Fig. 2.5   The zoom function makes it easy to make fine adjustments to a drawing

your own illustrations with a paint program is only a practical proposition if you have plenty of time available to draw up the illustrations, or you only require some pretty simple drawings.

Clip-Art

If you do not have the necessary skills to produce your own art-work, there is an alternative in the form of clip-art. This is merely predrawn material covering every conceivable subject. The drawings are stored in files on floppy disks so that they can be loaded into suitable d.t.p. programs, paint programs, and possibly other types of graphics program. It is quite common for graphics programs to have a certain amount of clip-art available as optional extras. There are also independent "third party" companies that produce clip-art for use with the popular d.t.p. programs.

The clip-art supplied with graphics programs is usually of excellent quality, but the range of subjects covered is not likely to be vast. This reveals the main problem with clip-art. There

30

must be an almost limitless range of subjects that users will require, and there is no way that even a very generous amount of sample clip-art can cover all requirements. In fact there is no way that a company with an extremely large catalogue of clip-art can cover all eventualities.

Unless you can afford to have custom clip-art drawn up, which few people can seriously contemplate, you will probably need to compromise over the artwork from time to time. If you can not find exactly what you require, perhaps you can locate something that is just about close enough to your requirements. On the other hand, it is better to simply not bother rather than to settle for inappropriate artwork. Someone who has a paint program and the ability to draw up whatever artwork they need clearly have an enormous advantage over someone who is restricted to using clip-art.

It is perhaps worth mentioning that there is plenty of PD (public domain) and shareware clip-art available for the PCs in a number of popular graphics program formats. Although PD and shareware software often tend to be grouped together as though they were exactly the same, they are actually totally different concepts. In both cases you pay what is usually only about £2.00 to £3.00 per disk to the supplier, but you are only paying for the disk itself plus a copying fee. In the case of PD software the author has decided not to claim copyright on his or her work, and it is available for anyone to use in any way they see fit, free of charge. This means that you are free to modify the material and use it as often as you like.

Shareware is a totally different concept, and is supplied on a "try before you buy" basis. Normally this type of software is in the form of a program which you try out over an evaluation period of up to about one month. If you decide to go on using the program you register your copy by sending the requested fee to the author. This fee is usually somewhat below the asking price for comparable commercial software. There may be some advantage in registering (apart from peace of mind for your honesty). This is often in the form of a proper manual to replace the on-disk operating instructions, plus perhaps a copy of a more advanced version of the program. In a clip-art context, you get the items of clip-art on the disk, and you are required to register if you should decide to go ahead and actually use some of it in earnest. Whether you are expected to pay for the lot or only the items you actually use depends on the artist's conditions. You have to check these, which are to be found in a text file on the disk.

If you can find suitable clip-art in an appropriate format for your graphics software, and at a price you can afford, then it offers a reasonably quick and straightforward solution to the problem. In practice you might find it difficult to satisfy all these criteria for all of your requirements. Possibly the best solution is to use clip-art where possible, but to resort to the do-it-yourself approach with a paint program when suitable clip-art can not be obtained.

Vector Graphics

With a pixel graphics system the drawing is stored in the computer's memory as a sort of map, with a small section of memory being used to indicate what is at each screen position, even if it is only black. Vector graphics programs are very different, and drawings are stored using a high resolution co-ordinate system. The resolution in which drawings are stored varies from one program to another, but it is generally about one hundred thousand by one hundred thousand, or more. Many vector graphics programs can operate with co-ordinates of many millions on each axis. Such high resolution precludes having the drawing stored in memory as a pixel style bit map. Even for a monochrome display this would require many megabytes of memory.

Instead, the drawing is stored in memory as a list of drawing elements. A line would be stored in memory as three pieces of information, coded in a manner selected by the programmer. First there would be the code number for a line, then the co-ordinate for one end of the line, and finally the co-ordinate for the other end of the line. A circle would be coded in a similar fashion, with first the circle code number, then the co-ordinate for the centre of the circle, and finally a value indicating the diameter of the circle. Any drawing elements (arcs, text, etc.) can be coded and stored in memory in a similar fashion. In practice things might be more complex than this, with additional information such as line widths and layer numbers having to be included. However, this does not affect the basic way in which things are handled, it just means that more information for each element in a drawing has to be coded and stored in memory.

The advantage of this method is that it enables drawings to be stored with resolutions that are as high as the application demands, rather than having the screen display set the limit. Obviously the drawings can not be displayed at their full resolution on the monitor's screen. The program processes each element stored in memory, and produces the screen display from this information. It has to work out a display that is as accurate as the screen resolution permits. The important point to note here, is that when a drawing is printed or plotted out, the program is not limited by the screen resolution. It again takes each element of the drawing, and produces it as accurately as possible on the hard copy. The accuracy with which the program stores the drawing is likely to be very much greater than the resolution of any current output device. Therefore, the quality of the hard copy is limited by the resolution of the printer or plotter, not by any constraints imposed by the program.

In theory you can produce drawings as complex as you like with a vector based graphics program, but in practice there will be some very definite limitations on what can be achieved. The first point to bear in mind is that the resolution of many output devices is not very high. A printer which operates at 120 dots per inch and prints out to a maximum size of 10 inches by 8 inches has a maximum resolution of 1200 by 960 dots. This is comparable to some high resolution monitors. If drawings take considerably less than the maximum printing area, then this effectively reduces the resolution of the printer. At 3 inches by 2 inches for instance, it would provide an effective resolution of 360 by 240 dots. This is comparable to low/medium resolution displays.

There are two points to note here. One is simply that the quality of the printout will not be very good at 120 d.p.i. For good quality graphics there is a lot to be said in favour of a resolution of 300 d.p.i. or more. The second point is that the amount of information that can be put into a drawing reproduced at this sort of resolution is strictly limited. There is no point in drawing up a complex piece of artwork which will just be a lot of incomprehensible lines and smudges when printed out. The larger the drawing can be printed, the more complex it can

33

be made. Where a small drawing is needed it is usually better to print it out twice the required size and then have it photo-reduced. This gives a much better perceived quality, with (say) a 180 d.p.i. printer effectively operating as a 360 d.p.i. type.

Pan and Zoom

There is clearly a difficulty in getting complex drawings into the computer in the first place. Although the program can handle very high resolutions, the display can not. On the face of it, this prevents you from clearly seeing on the screen the drawing you are producing. In a way this is true, and I have produced numerous drawings which, when viewed in their entirety on the screen, really look like little more than random dots and lines! This limitation is overcome using the program's pan and zoom facilities.

The zoom facility enables a small part of a drawing to be displayed across the whole screen so that even fine detail shows up clearly, and can be easily added to the drawing. The pan facility enables the part of the drawing that is being viewed to be altered. This is similar to the zoom facilities of many paint pro-grams. However, these facilities are usually much more sophis-ticated on vector drawing programs. In most cases you can zoom-in on any desired area of the drawing, and can zoom-in on a very small area indeed if desired.

The important point to note is that by zooming in you get a much clearer and more detailed view of that area of the drawing. This is because the program will display that part of the drawing to the best of the display's ability. It is not like "fat bit" editing where the zoomed view shows no more detail, but simply shows outsize pixels. Figure 2.6 shows a drawing in the Autosketch program, while Figure 2.7 shows a greatly zoomed view of a small part of the drawing. Notice how the zoomed view is sharp and detailed, whereas the zoomed view in DP2 is very coarse and lacking in detail.

The pan and zoom facilities greatly enhance the capabilities of vector based drawing programs, enabling complex drawings that would otherwise be impractical to be produced with reasonable ease. Although it might seem that these facilities totally remove any limitations on the maximum size and complexity of draw-ings, things are not really quite as simple as this. The first

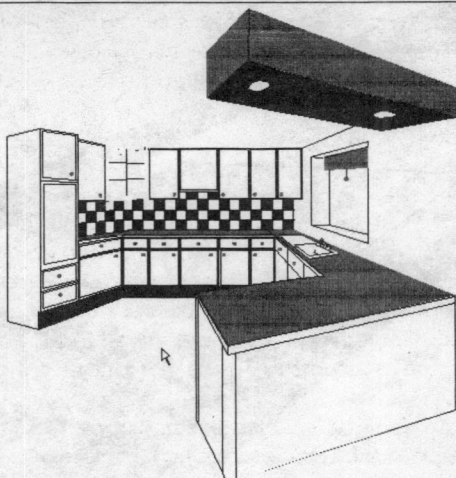

Fig. 2.6   A kitchen interior — an Autosketch demonstration drawing

problem is that panning and zooming takes a vast amount of complex calculations in order to convert the details of the drawing elements stored in memory into an appropriate screen display. This means that you can sit there watching the display for a considerable period of time before a new view is produced.

The time taken on pan and zoom operations depends on the complexity of the drawing, the operating speed of the computer, and how well or otherwise the program is written. Some systems can handle practically any pan or zoom operation in a second or two, while others take very much longer. In the early days of computer based drawing systems it was often a case of having a cup of tea while the "zoomed" screen was redrawn! Fortunately, most modern computer drawing systems are very much better than this. Even so, some complex drawings require so much panning and zooming that they become rather impractical to produce. A few vector drawing programs now offer multiple on-screen views of a drawing so that instead of repeatedly panning backwards and forwards between two zoomed views, you

35

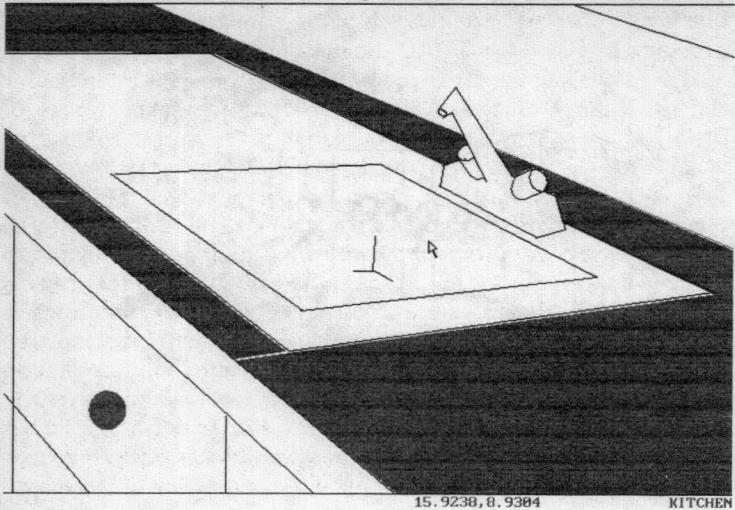

15.9238,8.9304   KITCHEN

*Fig. 2.7   A zoomed view of the kitchen interior, showing the sink area.
Note how this shows greater detail — not simply "fat bits"*

simply have them both on the screen at once, side-by-side or one
above the other. It is generally only the more expensive programs
that have this feature though.

It is best to be pragmatic about complex graphics. Rather
than spend large amounts of time drawing up a complex illustration that can not be printed out in sufficient detail, it would be
much better to split it into two drawings. These could be drawn
up much more quickly and easily, and printed out in greater
detail.

CAD or Illustration

As mentioned previously, vector graphics programs fall into two
main categories. These are the CAD (computer aided drafting)
and illustration programs. Although they may seem to be very
similar superficially, they are very different to use, and are aimed
at totally different users. There are a few programs which have
facilities that put them somewhere between the two types of

software, but even these programs tend to be heavily biased in one direction. Almost invariably they are basically illustration programs but with some CAD capabilities and features.

If we consider the CAD programs first, these are intended for the production of technical drawings, and are likely to be of little use for anything else. You can actually produce any type of drawing with good CAD programs, but they generally represent a relatively difficult (and possibly costly) method of producing business graphics, sketches, etc. The facilities offered by programs of this type are vast, and are far too numerous to be covered in detail here. There should be facilities for drawing straight lines of various thicknesses, circles, arcs, text in any size and at any angle, ellipses, polygons, and hatching enclosed areas. There should be on-screen rulers or grids plus a snap grid to make it easy to draw accurately to scale when necessary.

A good CAD program has excellent editing facilities. This is one respect in which a vector based program has a big advantage over a pixel based type. With a pixel based drawing program you can usually undertake editing such as copying or moving an area of screen to another part of the screen, but you can not pick out and edit individual drawing elements. If you select an area around (say) a circle, and move it to another position, you may take more than just the circle. If there is some text in the circle, then that will be moved along with the circle. If part of a line went through the circle, then this part of the line would be cut away from the rest of the line and moved!

Vector based drawing programs do not have this problem, since they have each drawing element stored in memory as a separate entity. You usually have the ability to pick out one element, or possibly a group of drawing elements, and to then move, copy, rotate, or rescale them. More basic editing commands permit individual end points of lines to be shifted, pieces of line to be trimmed away, and lines to be extended to meet other lines. The number of commands available with even the more simple CAD programs is quite large. In order to produce quite simple technical drawings you will need quite an array of commands at your disposal.

With some types of software that have large numbers of functions it is just a matter of finding and learning the ten or twenty percent of these functions that are actually of use to you.

37

Word processors are a good example of this. It is generally reckoned that most users only actually utilize about fifteen percent of the available functions, and ignore about eighty-five percent of them! With drawing programs the reverse is probably true. You will probably need to use about eighty or ninety percent of the available functions. It will inevitably take a fair amount of time in order to get everything set up and operating properly, and to learn to use the program efficiently. If you are going to use one of these programs properly you need to be fairly technically minded. Practically anyone can "doodle" with paint software, but it is much more difficult to produce something sensible using a CAD program. Presumably though, if you need to produce technical drawings using a CAD program, you will have a suitable scientific or technical background.

When dealing with CAD programs you will encounter references to "layers", and most CAD software can handle large numbers of layers. Layers are often likened to drawing using a pen on transparent film. Rather than drawing the whole thing onto one piece of film, you can draw different parts of the drawing onto different pieces of film. If you place the pieces of film one on top of the other, you can see the complete drawing. If some aspects of the drawing are not required, the appropriate piece or pieces of film are removed.

In a computer context I suppose it is true to say that the layers are notional rather than real. Each drawing element in the computer's memory is tagged with its notional layer number. If you switch off a layer, any element in the drawing having that layer number is ignored, and not displayed. This gives an effect much like the layers of transparent film analogy, and the same degree of control. In fact there is a greater level of control, because it is normally possible to shift elements of the drawing from one layer to another if desired. In a colour system a different colour is normally used for each layer so that you can see which layer each drawing element is on. Perhaps of greater importance, it makes it immediately apparent if you should start drawing something on the wrong layer. Layers are essential to some specialist types of drawing (such as printed circuit design), and can be useful for general illustration work. It is probably best not to use them just for the sake of it though. You would probably just confuse matters rather than making life easier.

Another standard feature of CAD programs is the ability to handle symbols. In this context symbols are pieces of predrawn artwork that can be called up from disk and added into drawings wherever you like, and as often as you like. In conventional drafting it is normal for stencils to be used where the same things must be drawn time and time again, in drawing after drawing. More recently rub-on transfers have been used for this type of thing. These both have the disadvantage of only being practical where something will have to be drawn a very large number of times. The cost of having custom stencils or rub-on transfers produced is normally too expensive unless something must be drawn up hundreds or even thousands of times.

The same is not true of CAD symbols where you can quickly draw up practically any desired symbol. There is no cost involved — only your time. Obviously symbols are not of use in all types of drawing, but for many types of technical drawing and illustration they can save massive amounts of time. Symbols are probably used most in diagrams, such as circuit diagrams (Fig. 2.8). However, they can be of value in many types of technical illustration.

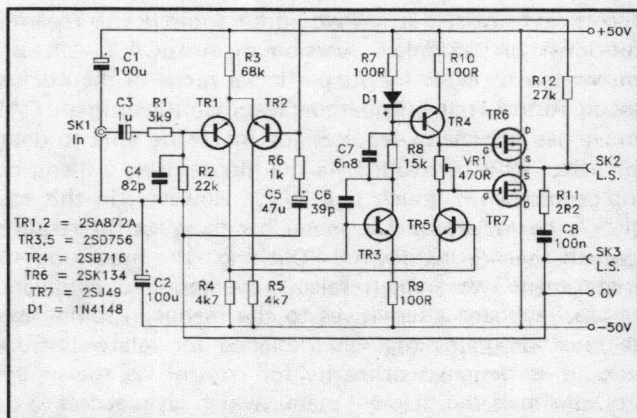

Fig. 2.8   Symbols are especially useful for drawings such as this circuit diagram, which is largely comprised of symbols

Some CAD programs are very expensive, and very sophisticated. These often have macro facilities. This enables repetitive tasks to be carried out largely automatically, which can save a lot of time (and tedium). Some programs go a stage further, and actually have programming languages which enable you to produce your own drawing commands. This type of thing can save vast amounts of time when undertaking many types of drawing. However, it takes a very long time to get the program customised and functioning just the way you want it. Coupled with the cost of these up-market CAD programs, and the technical know-how needed to get everything working properly, they can only be recommended for those who undertake large amounts of technical drawing. For the occasional user one of the simpler CAD programs, specifically designed for non-regular users, is a much more practical proposition.

Autosketch
Probably the best selling low cost CAD program is Autosketch, which tends to be regarded as a highly cut down version of the best selling up-market CAD program, AutoCAD. It does have some strong similarities to AutoCAD, but it is a purpose written program for those who require a quick and easy to use CAD program, rather than one with so many features that it takes a very long time to master it. It would be a mistake to regard it as a cut-down or "crippled" version of AutoCAD — it is a program written to cater for its particular niche in the market.

Although Autosketch is something less than the ultimate CAD program, it has too many features for me to be able to detail them all here. It is controlled via the mouse using a menu bar and drop-down menus, much like DP2. However, in this case you "click" the mouse on the menu bar to select the required menu, which then drops down. "Clicking" the mouse on the appropriate menu word then selects the required command.

There are keyboard alternatives to the menus in some cases, but like most programs that are designed for relatively infrequent use, it is designed primarily for control via the mouse.

Figure 2.9 shows the "Draw" menu, which gives access to the basic drawing elements. Figure 2.9 also shows some example drawing elements. In order to draw a line, having selected this item from the menu, you simply indicate the end points on the

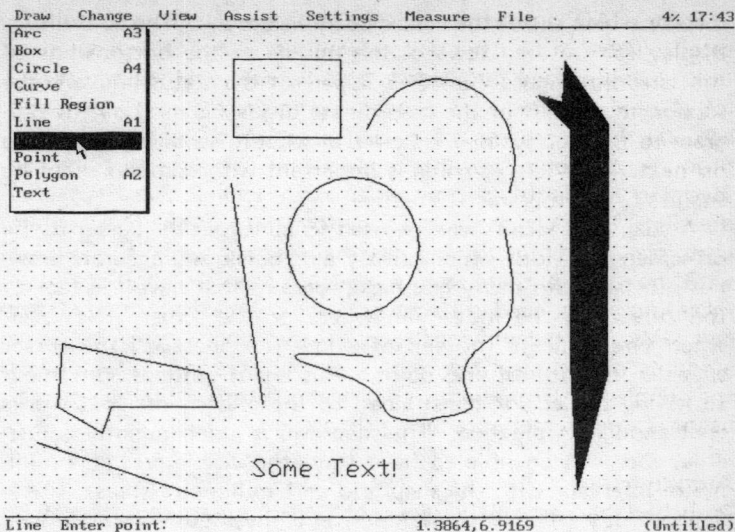

*Fig. 2.9   The "Draw" menu of Autosketch, together with some example
objects*

screen using the mouse and the on-screen pointer. Multi-segment
lines are catered for, and as you indicate more points, additional
segments are added in order to join up these points. "Clicking"
twice in the same place ends a line, and you can then start on the
next one. Circles are also easy to draw, and it is just a matter of
indicating the centre plus any point on the circumference. All
the drawing elements can be produced in this simple point 'and
"click" fashion.

In order to help you navigate your way around the drawing
quickly and accurately, an on-screen grid of dots can be displayed, with a user selected distance between adjacent dots. This is
the equivalent of conventional drafting on translucent film
placed over a grid sheet (like graph paper), with the backing sheet
acting as a sort of built-in ruler.

Some CAD programs offer the alternative of on-screen rulers
and pointers to aid measurements, but this seems to be much less
popular than a grid. Most CAD programs have a co-ordinate

41

display which shows the cursor position though. The co-ordinate display can be seen towards the middle of the bottom line of the screen in Figure 2.9. This is part of the status line, and the section to the left of the co-ordinate display is used by the program to tell you what it is doing, or what it is waiting for you to do next. This sort of thing is important with complex software such as CAD programs.

A snap grid facility can be used to constrain the cursor to the on-screen grid dots, which greatly aids quick and accurate drawing. In fact with many graphics programs that have this facility the cursor can be moved anywhere on the screen. However, when you indicate the end of a line (or whatever) the cursor snaps to the nearest grid point. This is not quite as convenient as having the cursor constrained to the grid points, but works well enough in practice. The snap grid is independently adjustable, and it is possible to have (say) the visible grid at 4 millimetre intervals, with the snap grid at 1 millimetre steps. This is a good way of arranging things as it gives quite fine control, but avoids having the display obscured by masses of grid dots. The scaling is user definable incidentally, and the notional page size can be 1 millimetre square, 100 miles by 80 miles, or anything you like.

The snap grid will not always provide fine enough control of the cursor. One way around this is to zoom in on the appropriate area of the drawing and set a much finer grid. Alternatively, co-ordinates can be typed in from the keyboard. This enables drawing points to be placed wherever you like, and with great accuracy (to several decimal points if necessary). This completely avoids any restrictions on drawing accuracy due to the limitations of the display's resolution. Apart from straightforward absolute co-ordinates, it is possible to use relative types. The standard form of relative co-ordinate is in the form of so many units along and so many up/down from an existing point. Polar co-ordinates are a common alternative, and take the form of an offset from the existing point in a certain direction.

Editing

CAD programs, including the relatively simple ones such as Autosketch, offer excellent editing facilities. Figure 2.10 shows the "Change" drop-down menu. This offers simple facilities

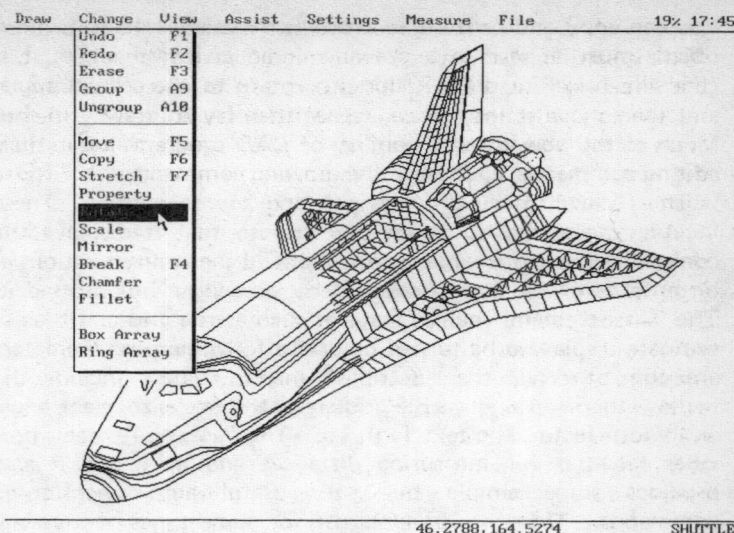

Undo   F1
Redo   F2
Erase   F3
Group   A9
Ungroup   A10

Move   F5
Copy   F6
Stretch   F7
Property
Rotate
Scale
Mirror
Break   F4
Chamfer
Fillet

Box Array
Ring Array

46.2788,164.5274   SHUTTLE

*Fig. 2.10   Screen dump showing the Autosketch "Change" menu. Much
of a CAD program's power lies in its editing facilities*

such as moving an object to a new position, erasing items, copying them, and changing them to a different layer. The "Undo"
and "Redo" commands are very useful ones which, with
Autosketch anyway, enable virtually any command to be
reversed, and then reinstated again if desired. Editing as well as
drawing commands can be reversed. Editing commands normally
operate on one object at a time, but objects can be grouped
together and edited en masse if desired. The group can be
broken down into individual objects again ("Ungrouped") if
desired. This is a powerful feature which enables a couple of
editing commands to achieve what might otherwise require
dozens of commands.

Further editing commands enable mirror images of objects to
be generated, and for objects to be increased/decreased in size
("Scaled"), or rotated by a specified number of degrees. Some
of these facilities might not seem terribly useful, but they should
not be underestimated. Having drawn up something like a bolt,

you can copy and resize it to produce other sizes of bolt. If an object must appear in a drawing at an awkward angle, it is generally easier to draw it upright, rotate to the correct angle, and then move it into place, rather than try to draw it in-situ. Much of the power and flexibility of CAD programs lies in their editing commands, and not in the drawing commands.

The "View" menu provides pan and zoom facilities. These include the ability to zoom the view so that it displays the complete drawing as large as possible, and the ability to zoom in on an area of the screen selected by drawing a box around it. The "Assist" menu enables features such as the grid and the co-ordinate display to be turned on and off. Numerous parameters are controlled via the "Settings" menu. These include the scaling, the snap and visible grid sizes, the text size, slant angle and width factor, the text font, etc. The "Measure" menu provides facilities for measuring distances and area, and it also provides some simple but very useful auto-dimensioning commands. These are of little use for some types of drawing, but are obviously very useful indeed for most machine drawing, house plans, etc. Finally, the "File" menu is used for such things as saving a drawing to disk, loading an existing drawing for editing, printing and plotting drawings, etc.

As should be apparent from this brief description, although Autosketch is a relatively simple CAD program, it is a complex piece of software and is very powerful. In fact it has more features than I have been able to mention here, and it can handle most drawing tasks.

3D CAD

Some form of three dimensional capability is a feature of many medium priced and up-market CAD programs. The sophistication of the three dimensional capabilities varies enormously, and in general you get what you pay for. Some have what are often termed two and a half dimensional facilities. The drawings produced are three dimensional in that they are proper three dimensional views. In fact they are isometric views in most cases. This is a convenient but slightly non-scientific form of three dimensional view. The drawings are two dimensional in that there are only "X" and "Y" dimensions, with no true "Z" dimension being used. What this means in practice is that you draw up a three dimensional view, and that is the only view you get. If you need a view from a different side, you must start again.

Even if a CAD program does not have any two and a half or three dimensional capability, you can still draw up three dimensional views of things. However, without any assistance from the program this will probably be rather difficult. The end results are likely to be sketches and not accurate scale drawings.

With true three dimensional drawing programs you supply X, Y, and Z co-ordinates for each end of every line, arc, etc., in the drawing. It is then possible to view the drawing from any angle and distance. You are putting into the computer an accurate three dimensional model of the subject, and then generating as many different views as you need from this computerised model. A few programs, particularly those intended for architectural use, actually let you view the drawing from the inside! Apparently the idea is to draw up a room, complete with furnishings, and then let clients see what it will look like from the inside. Again, you can have several different views looking from different viewpoints and in different directions.

The more simple three dimensional CAD programs are of the so-called "wire frame" variety. In other words, the objects depicted in the drawing are simple "see through" frames and do not have any proper surfaces. Other programs have hidden line removal facilities that give the impression of solid surfaces. Figure 2.11 shows an example of a 3D wire frame drawing, while Figure 2.12 shows the same drawing with hidden line removal (this is one of the AutoCAD demonstration drawings). At the top end of the market there are true surface modelling programs which give shaded surfaces, and an extremely realistic effect. In some cases the CAD program does not have these shading facilities built-in, but can have the drawings it produces processed by a separate shading or "rendering" program.

Three dimensional CAD programs can produce some very impression looking results, but this type of drawing is not something to be undertaken lightly. Most programs of this type are quite expensive, and many of them will only run properly on some quite sophisticated and costly hardware. The main problem is that they are quite difficult to master. Even with two dimensional drawing programs there tends to be a sort of mental

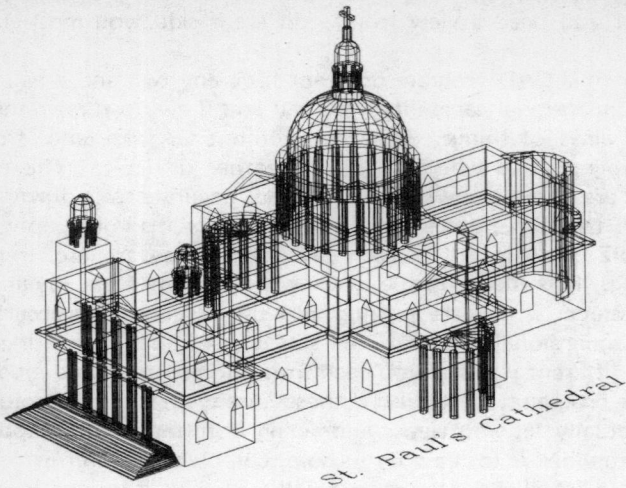

Fig. 2.11   The wire frame version of an AutoCAD demonstration drawing

block when you first use them. This is not really surprising, since after spending a lifetime drawing using pens, pencils, and paper, the switch to a mouse and a monitor screen is a large one. After some experience with a drawing program though, most people get used to the new way of doing things. Presumably, over a period of time the computer system becomes the normal way of drawing, while pencil and paper become quite alien!

With three dimensional drawing programs there is the additional problem of having to think in three dimensions while actually working on a two dimensional display. Even if you are used to using two dimensional CAD programs, this is still quite a leap for the mind. Three dimensional CAD programs provide help in making this leap, such as multiple views of the drawing, but it still requires a lot of effort and skill on the part of the draughtsman. This type of drawing is really a very specialised area of computer graphics, and one that the occasional user might never master.

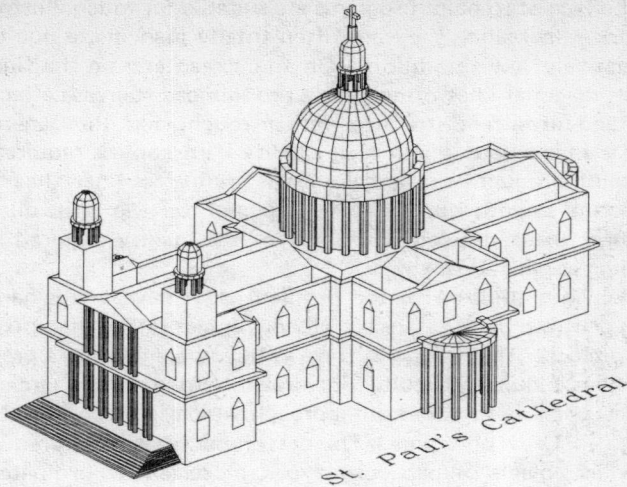

Fig. 2.12   The same drawing as Figure 2.11, but with hidden line removal

Illustration Programs

As already pointed out, illustration programs are vector based drawing programs, like CAD software. On the other hand, to use they are often much more reminiscent of paint programs than CAD programs. This is something that depends on the particular program concerned, and an illustration program that is designed primarily for producing technical illustrations will have strong similarities to CAD programs. Most illustration programs are not primarily designed for this type of thing though, and they have the emphasis on free-hand drawing facilities (like paint programs), rather than drawing to scale using straight lines, circles, etc. I would not wish to give the idea from this that there are no straight line and circle functions in illustration programs. They are generally equipped with a reasonable range of drawing tools. The drawing facilities of this type generally fall well short of CAD standards, but the free-hand drawing facilities tend to be much superior.

47

On the face of it, paint programs are suitable for much illustration work. In reality they are often totally inadequate due to their relatively low resolution. On the screen and on the final printout, diagonal lines often have a pronounced staircase effect. Circles and arcs tend to look rather rough, and the general quality is inadequate where high quality hard copy is required. Some paint programs do actually have printer routines that to some extent smooth out the "rough edges" on the print outs, but usually these still fall well short of the quality required in demanding applications.

The obvious solution to the problem is to have a free-hand drawing program that uses vector based graphics rather than pixel based graphics. This is fine in theory, but implementing a practical system is quite difficult. For drawing straight lines, circles, etc., it is possible to adopt an approach which is much like the one used in CAD programs. The drawing entities are stored in memory as objects of particular types, at certain co-ordinates, and of a certain size. They are then reproduced on the screen, printer, or whatever, at the maximum resolution of the device concerned.

The main problem is in achieving a method of free-hand drawing that will give a very high quality output on suitable printers and plotters. It is easy enough to have a program that lets you draw on the screen in paint program fashion, but how is this relatively low resolution drawing then converted into high quality hard copy. As pointed out previously, there are routines that can give "smoothed" printed output from paint programs, but these routines are not totally successful. It would be unreasonable to expect a program to invent added resolution and to always get it right.

The usual solution adopted in illustration programs is to use Bezier curves. The best way to learn about Bezier curves is to experiment with a suitable illustration program for a few minutes. It soon becomes very obvious and easy to get the exact curve you require. I can explain the basic principle here, but this may make it all seem a bit more cumbersome than it really is. A Bezier curve is controlled by two lines, one at each end of the curve. The angles of the lines set the start and finish directions of the curve. The lengths of the lines control the sharpness of the curve. A short line gives a sharp curve initially, followed by

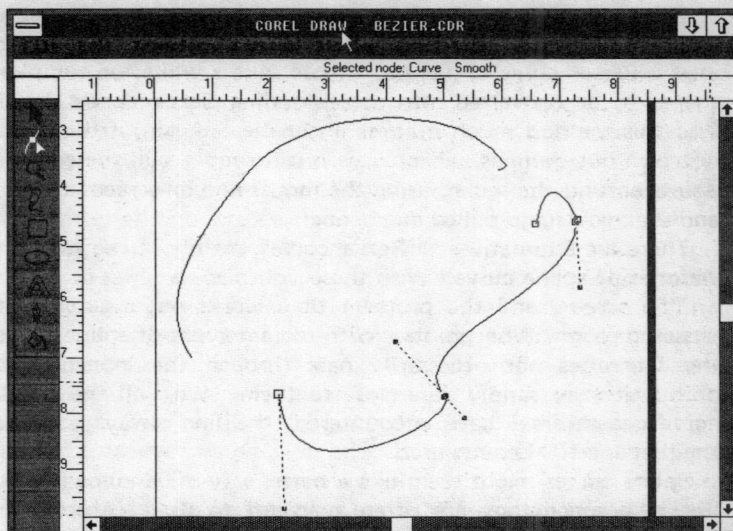

Selected node: Curve   Smooth

Fig. 2.13   Two multiple Bezier curves. Some of the control lines and points are shown for the lower curve

relatively straight line. A long line gives a long steady curve, and together they give tremendous control over the curve, permitting complex shapes to be produced with just a single Bezier curve. Figure 2.13 shows some example Bezier curves, complete with some control lines. Of course, normally the control points and lines would optionally be shown on the screen for editing purposes, but would not appear on the hard copy.

Although one Bezier curve can be manipulated into some complex shapes, practical drawings often require such complex shapes that a single Bezier curve can not accommodate them. The solution to this problem is to have two or more Bezier curves joined end to end. This permits any curve to be accurately reproduced. With some programs you have to produce the Bezier curves by indicating the control points, which can then be dragged around the screen if the curve produced was not as expected.

Alternatively, some programs let you draw free-hand on the screen, and the shape you have drawn is automatically converted into a Bezier curve or curves. It can take a while for complex shapes to be converted into corresponding Bezier curves, but I find this method much quicker and easier. Again, if things do not turn out quite as expected, you can simply pull the control points around the screen using the mouse and on-screen pointer, and soon get things pulled into shape.

There are alternatives to Bezier curves, mainly in the form of varieties of spline curve. With these you place a series of points on the screen, and the program then works out a curve that passes through these points. With certain types of spline curve the line does not necessarily pass through the intermediate points, it may simply pass close to them. With all the spline curve generators I have encountered, the line always touches the first and final points used.

Spline curves might seem like a better way of handling things, but in practice they are often awkward to use. In order to define a complex curve accurately it is often necessary to indicate a large number of points. In fact it can often be necessary to put down a large number of points in order to produce relatively simple shapes. This can make it relatively slow and difficult to indicate a rough initial shape, and more time-consuming to edit it into precisely the required shape. The main problem is that spline curves generally tend to be a bit unpredictable.

The most predictable types are the ones that produce lines with a minimum of curvature, which pass through the points placed on the screen. These tend to give something not far removed from a series of straight lines at angles to one another. For many types of drawing this gives unsatisfactory results. The spline curves that give smoother results generally give a much better final product, but are difficult to predict because the line does not usually pass through the intermediate points, and in some cases might not actually pass all that close to them.

Bezier curves enable complex shapes to be produced using a minimum number of control points, and once a basic shape has been produced it is possible to quickly and easily "fine tune" it. Things are especially easy with the programs which enable you to draw onto the screen, and which then work out suitable

Bezier curves for you. Matters are far less straightforward if you have to work out the positions of the control points for yourself. However, with practice most users soon learn to work efficiently using this method.

Fills

A common and important feature of illustration programs is some form of "fill" facility. At its most basic level this just consists of a command that enables an indicated area of the drawing to be filled in with the desired colour (or shade of grey if you are working in monochrome). Most fill facilities go well beyond this basic level though. Often it is possible to fill areas with complex patterns. This is a feature of many paint programs incidentally, and I suppose that the hatching feature of many CAD programs is comparable to this.

Perhaps the most useful type of fill is the graduated type, or a "fountain" fill as it is sometimes called. With these the colour of the fill varies from a specified start colour to a specified finishing colour. In a black and white system the graduation is between two selected shades of grey (or from black right through to white). A typical application of a fountain fill would be to produce a background that went from (say) light yellow at the top, through orange to deep red at the bottom. This type of thing tends to give more lively and pleasing results than a background of a single colour.

Most programs that have this feature enable the direction of the graduation to be specified. In other words, the colour change does not have to be from top to bottom; it can be from side to side or diagonally at any desired angle. In most cases there is also a radial graduation option. This has the start colour at the centre, and the finishing colour around the edges. There may even be a facility to permit the centre to be offset somewhat from the centre of the drawing element being filled. A typical use for a graduated radial fill is to give a circle a three dimensional look. In effect, using a radial graduated fill on a circle converts it into a sphere. Figure 2.14 shows some example graduated fills.

Illustration programs do not usually provide much help in producing three dimensional views. It is assumed that the user will have sufficient artistic ability to handle the perspective, etc., properly. There are often a few aids though, and probably the

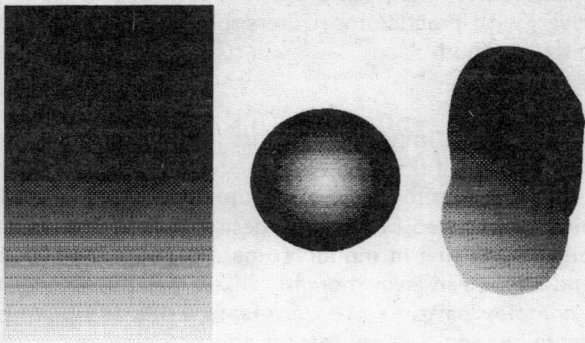

Fig.2.14   Some examples of graduated fills, including a radial type

most useful of these is the ability to stack up objects one in front of the other. As a simple example, suppose that you draw up a front view of a car. You could then make a slightly smaller copy of this, and offset it slightly to one side. Most illustration programs permit groups of drawing objects to be selected and rescaled in this way. You could repeat this operation a few times, producing a series of car drawings of diminishing size, and increasingly offset from the original.

As it stands, all this gives you is a confusing mass of overlapping and intermingled car drawings that would probably not look like anything much at all. However, if the car drawings are stacked in sequence, with the largest at the front and the smallest at the rear, you get what looks like a line of cars tailing off into the distance. The program provides all the necessary hidden line and shading removal, so that objects towards the rear do not show through those towards the front. There may be a limit on the number of objects that can be stacked in this way, but normally this limit is quite large. Figure 2.15 shows an example of stacking.

Fig. 2.15   *Using stacking to give a simple 3D effect. The program removes hidden lines and shading*

Another powerful feature of most illustration programs is their text handling capabilities. Apart from having numerous different fonts available in practically any desired size, there are usually facilities to permit clever things to be done with the text strings, or possibly with individual characters in each piece of text. Just what can be achieved varies considerably from one illustration program to another, but these are some typical facilities. Fills and graduated fills can be used on text strings or applied to characters separately.   In other words you could have a text string graduated from (say) yellow on the first letter, through green in the middle, ending up with blue on the last letter. Alternatively, each individual character could have this yellow to blue graduation.

Further facilities permit the shapes of characters to be altered. One way in which this can operate is to have the text characters, in effect, as normal graphics shapes with control points. By moving the control points you can alter the shape of any text character in any desired fashion.   It is also possible to shift individual characters, either for manual kerning purposes, or for special effect. Individual control of the size of characters can be used to provide some interesting effects.   The letters could be small initially, gradually getting larger towards the end of the text string. An advanced feature of some illustration programs permits text to be wrapped around a graphics object, or perhaps even around a large text character.

For technical drawings and some other applications this type of thing is obviously not of great use. For advertising and many general illustration purposes it is very useful though, and permits an imaginative designer to produce some stunning results relatively quickly and easily. For some types of single page document where many people are using desk top publishing (d.t.p.) programs, an illustration program would probably be a much better choice. Where graphics and a limited amount of fancy text is needed, an illustration program is almost invariably the most appropriate type of program to use.

A really good illustration program is probably the best type of drawing program for general illustration work. They can handle just about any drawing task (within reason), and can produce very high quality results. There are a few drawbacks, one of which is that this type of software is very demanding on the hardware. Powerful illustration programs require fast 16-bit computers with good displays.

Until recently there were few programs of this type to choose from, even if you had a suitably powerful computer. This situation has changed in recent times, and for PCs there is now a reasonable range of illustration software from which you can select the program that best suits your needs. Illustration software is not as difficult and time-consuming to learn to use as CAD software, but it is far less straightforward to use than paint programs. You can usually learn to produce some simple illustrations in a fairly short time, but it might take quite a while before the program is fully mastered. If you will be doing a reasonable amount of illustration work, it is likely to be well worth the effort required in order to learn every aspect of such a program.

Corel Draw!
There are several popular illustration programs for the PCs, but "Corel Draw!" is probably the most popular and best known program of this type. Like DP2, it makes use of both icons and drop down menus. The icons are used to select the main drawing functions, while the menus give access to functions such as saving and loading drawings, 3D effects, etc. Figure 2.16 shows a Corel Draw! screen dump, complete with a demonstration

Fig. 2.16   A Corel Draw! screen dump showing the preview screen and the rulers

drawing loaded.   The icons can be seen down the left-hand edge of the screen, and you will also notice that the optional "rulers" are activated.

You will further notice that the drawing is displayed on the screen twice.   The left-hand section of the screen is the normal editing area, which is used for working on the drawing.   This is something less than a full WYSIWYG display though, and it does not show any fills or any colours for example.   However, it does enable the program to operate reasonably fast.

The right-hand section of the display is the preview screen, which shows, as far as possible, an accurate representation of the drawing, complete with colours, hidden line removal, and fills. Even though the screen dump is a black and white type, the differences between the editing and preview displays show up quite well.   Changes to drawings can take quite a long time to be drawn on the preview screen.   To save time it can be switched off, and called up periodically so that the drawing can be checked. Alternatively, it can be "frozen", and only updated from time to time. It can also be enlarged to fill the whole screen if desired, so that a more detailed view of the drawing is provided.

If we now briefly consider each of the icons in turn, starting at the top, the first one selects the editing mode where individual points in an object can be moved around. For example, if you have drawn a free-hand line on the screen, and it is not quite as desired, this mode enables the line to be (literally) pulled into shape using the mouse to move the control points. The next icon selects an alternative editing mode which permits complete objects to be selected and then moved, stretched, squashed, or edited in some way. The third icon (the magnifying glass) gives access to the pan and zoom facilities. Incidentally, the preview screen can be independently panned and zoomed if desired.

The next icon (a pencil) permits drawing of straight lines or free-hand drawing. For free-hand drawing you simply hold down the mouse button and move the mouse/pointer around. This is not quite like drawing with a paint program, where the line appears as you move the mouse/pointer. In this case, once you have finished drawing a line, the program works out a suitable Bezier curve (or curves), and the line is then drawn on the screen. With a complex line it can take a significant time for the line to be calculated and drawn. Straight lines are produced by "clicking" the mouse at the start and finish points.

Boxes, circles, and ellipses are drawn using the next two icons. These can be filled or empty, as desired. The seventh icon is used for adding text, and a massive range of text fonts (sets of character shapes) and sizes are available. Text can be edited in various ways once it is in place on the screen, further enhancing the possibilities. The last two icons permit the control of line widths, fill patterns, fill colours, etc. Control panels give considerable control over most parameters, and Figure 2.17 shows the control panel for graduated fills. Parameters can be entered from the keyboard if desired, but the figures are normally controlled using the mouse and the on-screen arrows. Pointing to an arrow that is aimed upwards and holding down a mouse button increments a value — pointing to an arrow that is aimed downwards and pressing the mouse button results in the value being decremented.

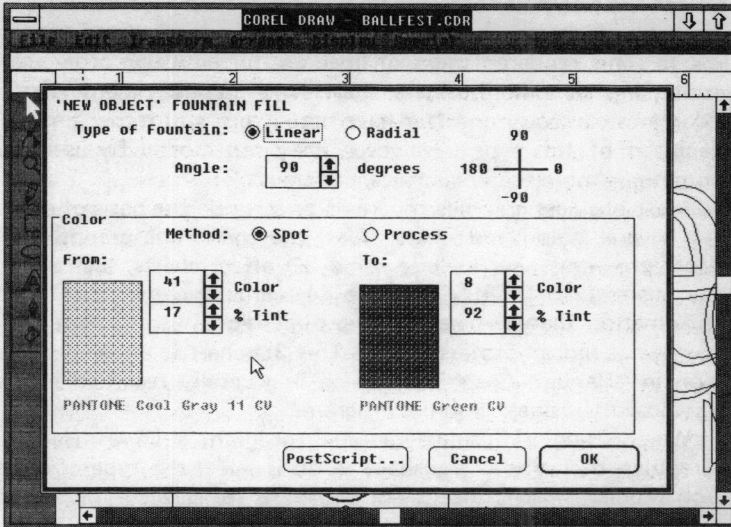

Fig. 2.17   The Corel Draw! control panel for graduated fills

With relatively few editing tools, Corel Draw! might seem to be a rather simple drawing program. This is not really the case though, and it has been deliberately designed to use a limited number of tools, with each one performing more than one task. This is much like conventional methods of producing artwork, and has made Corel Draw! popular with those who are used to traditional methods of generating artwork. It makes the program fairly easy to learn and use on a superficial level, but a fair amount of time and effort is required in order to master all the program's complexities. Current versions of the program have some quite sophisticated 3D effects for example, and learning to fully exploit these can take some time. Learning to fully exploit a powerful program such as this should be well worth the effort though.

Business Graphics
The facilities available in business graphics programs vary greatly from one program to another, with similar variations in their

prices. In the past these programs have tended to offer little in the way of normal drawing facilities (for producing lines, circles, etc.). This rendered them of little use for anything other than producing standard business charts and graphs. Many of the programs currently on offer have better, but still rather limited, facilities of this type. However, they can mostly be used for something more than pie charts, bar charts, etc.

Most business graphics programs operate on the basis of offering several graph and chart types (pie chart, line graph, etc.). Most programs now include some 3D effect charts, such as 3D pie charts (Fig. 2.18). These do not actually convey any more information than the normal two dimensional variety, but look somewhat more "professional". This 3D chart is under production in "Harvard Graphics", which is generally regarded as the "standard" business graphics program.

When using a business graphics program such as Harvard Graphics, basically all you have to do is select the type of chart you require, answer a series of questions (to select the required text font, headings, etc.), and feed in the necessary data. Figure

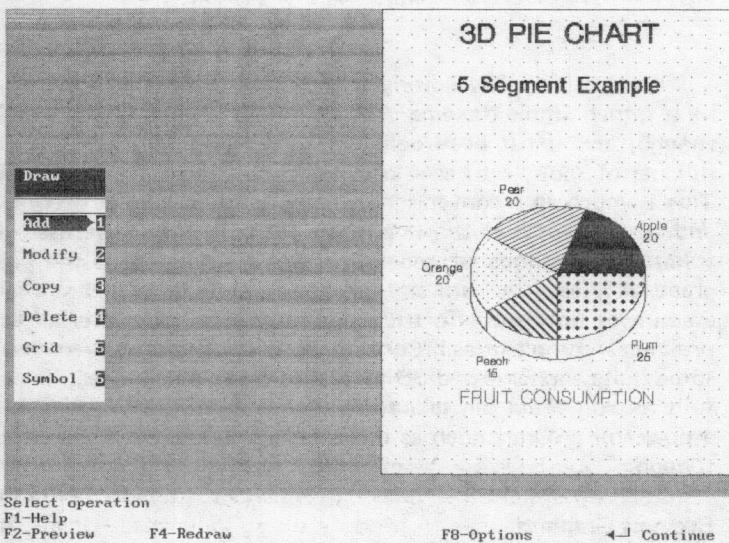

Fig. 2.18   A simple 3D pie chart being produced using "Harvard Graphics"

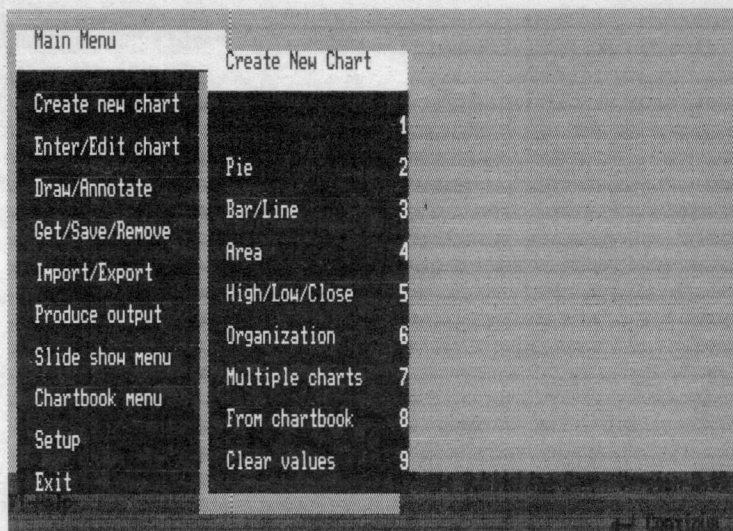

```
Main Menu
                  Create New Chart

Create new chart
                                        1
Enter/Edit chart
                  Pie                   2
Draw/Annotate
                  Bar/Line              3
Get/Save/Remove
                  Area                  4
Import/Export
                  High/Low/Close        5
Produce output
                  Organization          6
Slide show menu
                  Multiple charts       7
Chartbook menu
                  From chartbook        8
Setup
                  Clear values          9
Exit
```

*Fig. 2.19   The initial (and main) menu of Harvard Graphics, plus the
"Create New Chart" sub-menu*

2.19 shows the main menu and a sub-menu of Harvard Graphics,
while Figure 2.20 shows the screen which is used to feed data
into the program. This sample data produces the simple 3D pie
chart of Figure 2.18 incidentally. With this type of software you
are not drawing things in the same way as the other kinds of
program discussed in this chapter. You make decisions about the
type of chart, the headings, etc., supply the data, and then the
drawing is automatically generated from this. You do not need
to have any artistic ability or technical drawing know-how in
order to use a business graphics program effectively.

You can often embellish the chart produced with additional
labels, etc. With the more up-market programs such as Harvard
Graphics you have a wide choice of text fonts and sizes, and can
also add lines and other drawing elements to the chart or graph.
You may even be able to produce simple flow charts, logos, and
other simple illustrations. In some cases there is even a library
of predrawn artwork which can be used in your illustrations.

59

Title: 3D PIE CHART
Subtitle:
Footnote:

Slice	Label Name	Value Series 1	Cut Slice Yes No	Color	Pattern
1		20	No	2	1
2	Pear	20	No	3	2
3	Orange	20	No	4	3
4	Peach	15	No	5	4
5	Plum	25	No	6	5
6			No	7	6
7			No	8	7
8			No	9	8
9			No	10	9
10			No	11	10
11			No	12	11
12			No	13	12

| F1-Help | | | F9-More series |
| F2-Draw chart | F6-Colors | F8-Options | F10-Continue |

Fig. 2.20   The screen which is used for entering data into Harvard Graphics

Business graphics programs are basically somewhat simpler than most other types of graphics program, but there are still a lot of "extras" and variations available if you need them. As with practically all modern software, you need to carefully study the available features in order to find out which ones are of use to you.

It is worth mentioning that it is possible to produce business graphics using virtually any graphics program. It is generally easier and quicker using a business graphics program, since it will do much of the work for you. The price that generally has to be paid for this is somewhat less control over the final appearance of the chart.

It is also worth mentioning that programs such as accounting software, spreadsheets, and even databases, sometimes have what is effectively a built-in business graphics program. This means that it is often possible to produce the usual types of business chart without having to buy any separate business graphics program. This has to be regarded as the most convenient way of handling things, since the data for the charts will normally be in the program already. Producing the charts therefore takes a minimum amount of time and effort on the part of the user.

The drawback of this method is that the built-in graphics facilities of something like an accounting program are not likely to be as sophisticated as those of a business graphics program. Sometimes you can effectively have the best of both worlds by having a business graphics program that can import data from your spreadsheet, database, or whatever. Most business graphics programs have the ability to import data from some popular spreadsheet programs, etc. In most cases they can also export data to certain other programs, although this is probably a less useful feature than the import one.

Chapter 3

D.T.P. SOFTWARE

In terms of the facilities offered, and the method of use, there are considerable variations from one d.t.p. (desk top publishing) program to another. On the other hand, there are features and methods of working that are common to many d.t.p. programs. In this chapter we will consider some of the more common and important d.t.p. features, together with the basic ways in which these programs operate. Due to the marked differences in the way in which they operate it is necessary to explain them in fairly broad terms, with little that is specific to a particular d.t.p. program. Where a specific program is used as the basis for examples in this chapter, the program is Timeworks Publisher, which is an extremely popular mid-priced d.t.p. program.

Basics
The basic function of a d.t.p. program is to take some text, or some text and graphics, and to produce properly made up pages from them. Obviously text can be entered into a word processor and printed out, and as we have already seen, with some word processors it is even possible to add graphics into the text. As explained in Chapter 1, some word processors can even handle multiple columns.

Even the most powerful of word processors fall short of true d.t.p. standards though. With a d.t.p. program the pages can have complex multiple column arrangements if desired, text can be as large or as small as you like (within reason), and a large number of text fonts and styles are available. A word processor may well provide proportionally spaced text, but d.t.p. software should provide manual and automatic kerning (these terms are explained in detail later on). In fact with any reasonably good d.t.p. software you can make up pages of the type found in books, magazines, newspapers, etc. The limits are likely to be set more by your imagination than the limitations of the d.t.p. software.

Virtually all d.t.p. programs are designed to handle existing text files or graphics files stored on computer disks, rather than to have the text and graphics produced using the d.t.p. software itself. It is usually possible to type text into these programs, and in some cases there is some drawing capability. However, they do not provide facilities which compare with those of word processors or graphics programs. Entering text and graphics tends to be relatively slow and cumbersome. Editing facilities for both text and graphics are normally very limited.

The ability to enter and edit text is there mainly as a means of making corrections or minor alterations to the text once it has been loaded into the program, and not as the primary means of entering text. Similarly, the basic graphics facilities are only intended as a means of producing very simple diagrams, adding frames around imported graphics, and this type of thing. Any remotely complicated drawings normally have to be produced using a proper graphics program, and then loaded into the d.t.p. program.

Obviously it will not normally be sufficient to have just the d.t.p. software. It will need to be backed up by a word processor or text editor, and possibly one or more drawing programs. The latter will not be discussed here, as this topic was discussed in detail in Chapter 2. In theory, if you are making up pages using text supplied by other people on computer disks, you do not need a word processor or text editor. In reality you are likely to need one of these for producing odd pieces of text, and a simple text editor should be regarded as a minimum requirement.

Some computers are supplied complete with some form of text editor, or possibly even a sophisticated word processor. The software supplied with the computer might be all that you need, but most of the text editors that are included in the software bundled with computers are pretty basic, and not the most usable of programs. A low cost word processor or text editor is likely to be more practical. It is possible to obtain suitable public domain programs for the PCs, and the cost of these is just a few pounds (i.e. the cost of the disk plus a small copying fee, etc.). The difference between a word processor and a text editor incidentally, is that a word processor has facilities for organising the text into pages and printing it out. A text editor either lacks these facilities, or only has very limited pagination and printing facilities.

64

In the current context, all that is needed is a program that permits the text to be entered into the computer, edited as necessary, and then stored on a computer disk. A text editor is therefore quite adequate for most purposes. If you are going to produce long articles, books, or any large pieces of text, then a good quality word processor will almost certainly prove to be well worth the cost. A program of this type should make it as easy as possible to enter and edit large chunks of text.

A point to keep in mind is that the word processor or text editor must be capable of generating text files that can be loaded into the d.t.p. program. Most computers handle text in the form of standard code numbers, and this system of coding is known as ASCII (American Standard Codes for Information Interchange, and normally pronounced something like "asskey"). Any d.t.p. program should be capable of reading in text in this basic ASCII form. Most text editors product text in this form as standard, and most word processors can be made to produce ASCII text files.

With word processors there may be limitations on the way in which text can be formatted when producing ASCII files, but as we shall see shortly, this does not really matter. Formatting the text in the required manner using the word processor or the text editor is not normally necessary, and is unlikely to be the best way of doing things anyway.

Word processors sometimes save text to disk as simple ASCII files, but it is more normal for them to be saved as ASCII files plus some special formatting codes. In some cases the text and formatting instructions are all coded in a fashion that is unique to the particular word processor concerned. In either case, these can not be read into a d.t.p. program unless it has a facility specifically for reading in files produced by the word processor in question. It is not uncommon for d.t.p. programs to be able to read files in some common word processor formats. The d.t.p. program will usually respond to some basic formatting commands, and if a line of text is centred using the word processor, it will probably remain centred once it has been loaded into the d.t.p. program. This is not invariably the case though, and the d.t.p. program might simply strip off all the formatting commands, leaving what is essentially just a basic unformatted ASCII file.

Embedded Commands

Having loaded some text into a d.t.p. program, it is necessary to have some means of laying out the pages in the required manner. In fact this process does not necessarily start once the text has been loaded into the d.t.p. program, and can start at the word processor or text editor stage. As we have already seen, simple formatting commands used when preparing the text may be carried on into the d.t.p. program. This method only gives very limited capabilities though, and is of equally limited practical value.

A system used by some d.t.p. programs is to permit the use of embedded commands within the imported text. This permits great control over the finished document, enabling a full range of formatting commands to be used, text fonts, styles and sizes to be selected, etc. The exact manner in which this system is implemented varies from one d.t.p. program to another, but it generally works along the lines of using something like a couple of code letters to select the required command, possibly with some figures to provide additional information. As a couple of examples, the letters "CE" could be used to indicate that a line of text (a headline perhaps) should be centred in its column, or the code "FT15" could be used to indicate a change to font number 15. With a system of this type it is possible to control the format of the text before it ever reaches the d.t.p. program.

There is an obvious problem with this method of doing things in that the d.t.p. program must be able to distinguish between the text and the formatting commands. This is normally achieved by including a little used character as part of each embedded command. Most computer keyboards include several of these unusual characters, such as | , \, ¬ , and ~ , which can be used for this type of thing. These characters are not normally used in plain text, and there is little risk of a piece of text being mistaken for an embedded command. There is a slight risk of the character in question turning up in specialised material, such as scientific papers, d.t.p. book manuscripts, etc., but in these cases it must be omitted from the text initially. It can probably be added safely later, once the text has been loaded into the d.t.p. program and formatted.

A slightly different approach to the problem is to use something like a space and a fullstop at the start of each embedded command (e.g. " .CE"). This is something that would not normally occur in plain text. At the end of a sentence you would normally have some text characters followed by a full-stop and a space, but not the inverse of this. The advantage of such a system is that it does not put any text characters, even little used ones, "off limits".

Obviously with any system of this type there is a slight risk of text being interpreted as an embedded command. However, in practice this is not a major problem, and for the vast majority of users it is something that will never occur. If it should happen, it is likely to be as a result of an error when entering the text, rather than by the system being fooled.

D.T.P. Formatting

Embedded commands are not usually the sole method of formatting text. In order to get the page layouts looking just right it is normally necessary to resort to at least a small amount of editing in the d.t.p. program. I suppose that it would be possible to have a d.t.p. program that simply took in a word processor file with embedded commands, and then produced the hard copy from this.

The drawback of this system is that you would not see each page until it was printed out. Any changes would have to be implemented by going back to the original word processor file, seeking out the appropriate embedded commands, and making the appropriate alterations. Even a few small changes could result in every page having to be reprinted. Remember that changes to one page can have a knock-on effect which results in changes to every subsequent page. Using embedded commands as the only method of controlling the page layout, etc., would therefore be a rather slow and inconvenient way of handling things. Also, there are some aspects of page design which are more easily handled in the d.t.p. program than by using embedded commands.

It is normal for d.t.p. programs to give full control over the layout, fonts used, text size, etc., from within the program itself, even if embedded commands are supported. It is only fair to point out that by no means all d.t.p. programs do actually support embedded commands. Where embedded commands are implemented, it is probably quicker if they are used for some basic formatting of the documents. This will not always be possible, and it is something that is unlikely to be practical if you are making up documents from disk files received from a number of different sources. You might be able to get the co-operation of those who supply the disk files, but being realistic about it, this approach will probably not be practical. Many d.t.p. users do not prefer this method of working anyway. This is a matter of personal preference, and where a program offers different means of achieving the same thing it is always a good idea to try them all out to see which one suits you best.

When text is loaded into a d.t.p. program, the display normally shows the first page of text. We are assuming here that the program is one that can handle multi-page documents, which most of them can. It is only fair to point out that there are a few simple d.t.p. programs which are strictly one page at a time types, unsuitable for large documents. These are used in much the same way as the multi-page d.t.p. programs, but they must either be fed with no more text than they can handle in a single page, or they will simply clip off any text which will not fit onto the first (and only) page.

Unless the display is a very high resolution type, it will not be possible to see both the whole page, and an accurate representation of the page on a letter by letter basis. The vast majority of programs provide a WYSIWYG display, and the better the display quality, the more accurate the representation of the page should be. Like the preview facility of Wordperfect, a zoom facility normally permits part of a page to be examined in detail if desired. Figure 3.1 shows a zoomed view of a page in Timeworks, while Figure 3.2 shows the full view of the same page.

At this stage, any formatting commands carried through from the word processor, or demanded by embedded commands should be shown on the display. Otherwise there will just be a screenful of raw text, with no variations in font, text size, etc. To format the text in the desired manner it is largely a matter of indicating pieces ("blocks") of text that must be treated in some way. The method of selecting text and the required change varies from program to program, but these days most d.t.p. programs make heavy use of a mouse and pop-down menus. In most cases the commands can be selected via the keyboard shortcuts if preferred.

C:\PUBLISH\CH5DTP.DTP

CHAF

PC RE

There is an old joke about the woman who was
amazed that her old broom had lasted thirty years -
and it only needed two new handles and seven new
heads! I suppose that the modular construction of
PCs leaves them open to the same sort of claim.
Over the years you can put in a new display card

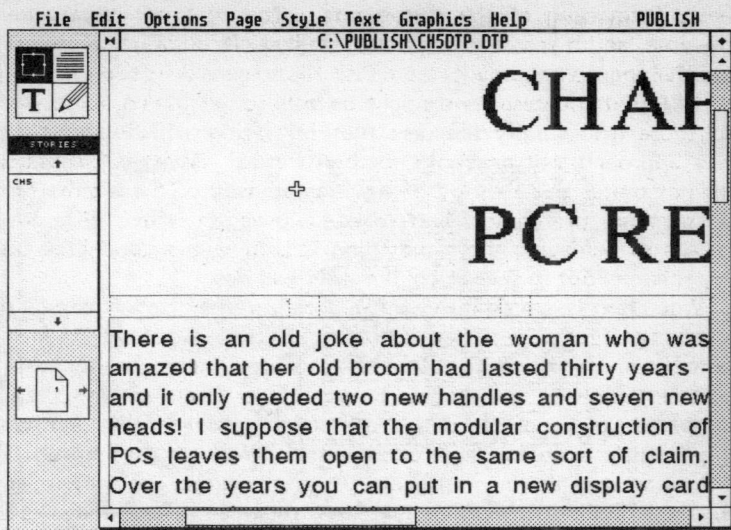

Fig. 3.1   A zoomed view enables a page to be viewed in great detail,
piece by piece

As a typical example of how text might be formatted in the
desired manner, the first task would probably be to select the
desired block of text. To do this the cursor is moved to the
beginning of the text that is to be processed and a button on the
mouse is depressed. Then the cursor is moved to the end of the
block of text, and the button is released. Timeworks uses a
quick and easy alternative, whereby the mouse is used to point
to the paragraphs of text which must be processed. Either way,
the selected block of text will be marked on the screen in some
way, so you can see that you have selected the right text, or that
a mistake has been made and a fresh attempt is required. There
may simply be marks left at the beginning and end of the block,
but more usually it would be shown in inverse video or in a
different colour to the rest of the text (Fig. 3.3).

Next the required change to the text is selected. Suppose that
the block of text that has been selected is actually a headline.
This will need to be larger than the main text, and will probably

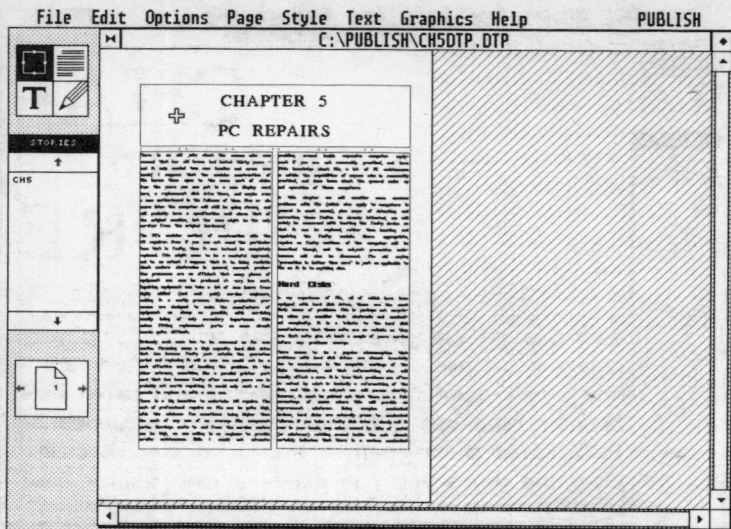

Fig. 3.2   The full page view does not show much detail, but it gives a good overall impression of the page layout

need to be in a different font as well. You would therefore select the font command, select the desired font from a list shown on the screen, and the text would then change to the new font.   Then the text size command would be issued, and the desired text size would be selected. The line of text would then change to the new, larger size.

With the text increased in size, it will obviously take up more space on the page. This is all handled by the d.t.p. program though, and the page is automatically adjusted to accommodate the larger text. This means that the text at the end of the page will be removed, and placed at the beginning of the next page. This will have a knock-on effect that will necessitate changes to all the subsequent pages, but the d.t.p. program will handle this automatically.

Having processed the headline satisfactorily, you would then move on to the main text, selecting the required font and text size again.   Then sub-headings could be selected, and perhaps

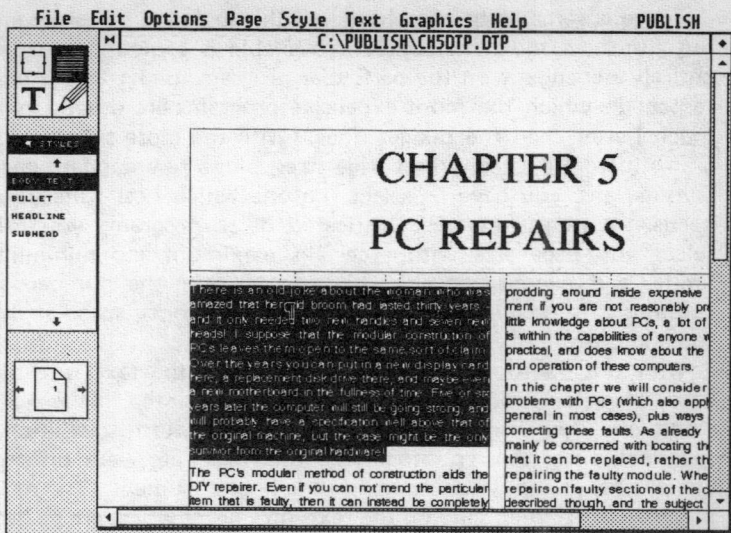

Fig. 3.3   The block of text to be edited is shown here in inverse video

changed to a slightly larger text size and centred within their columns. In this way the text can quickly and easily be formatted in the desired fashion, soon leaving you with the first page ready to print out.

Global Formatting

So far we have only considered the formatting of text in terms of such things as the text fonts and sizes used, whether or not lines are centred, and this type of thing. There is also the overall page layout to consider (the number of columns, the gap between them, how close the text is taken to the foot of the page, etc.). With any d.t.p. program there will be a default setup, with a certain number of columns, a certain gap at the foot of the page, a "standard" font which is used for text when it is first loaded, and so on. There are usually some on-screen marks to show the columns, and where loaded text will flow onto the page.

There is some ability to change all this in any d.t.p. program, but just how much flexibility is available is something that is entirely dependent on the particular program used. This is one respect in which the more expensive programs are usually very much better than the budget ones. With the more simple programs there are a few preset page sizes, plus a few standard page layouts, and you have to select the one which best suits your needs. With the most sophisticated d.t.p. programs you can select any page size within certain maximum and minimum limits, and exercise considerable control over the number of columns, the column width, the amount of empty space at the top and bottom of the page, etc.

With the traditional page make-up process the text is in the form of galley proofs, which have the text printed in the right fonts, sizes, etc., and with the right column width, but in one long column. Any photographs, drawings, etc., are printed actual size, as they must appear in the final document. The page make-up artist then cuts up the text into pieces which are pasted onto page layout sheets, together with any drawings and photographs. The adhesive used is normally a non-drying type so that items can easily be moved around. The layout sheets are marked with column markers and other marks to aid the artist in getting things accurately positioned.

Some d.t.p. programs permit things to be done in a fashion which is analogous to this traditional page make-up method. This is not a method that can be recommended for newcomers to making up pages though. It is something that is included primarily for those who are very experienced at this sort of thing. In particular, it is aimed at those who have been making up pages using the traditional paste-up method, and who wish to change over to d.t.p.

The more normal approach is to first select or design the basic page layout, including such things as the number of columns, gap at the bottom of each page, the position of page numbers, and any headings to be included at the top of each page. The text is then loaded, and will flow into the columns. As explained previously, any formatting of the text that results in it expanding, such as changing headings into a larger text size, results in the text being automatically shuffled around to suit the new scheme of things. If you should change your mind and change the headings back to a smaller size, then the text will again be shuffled to fit the revised scheme. This is much easier and quicker than moving things around yourself.

Frames

This automatic adjustment of the text will normally take place when any significant changes are made to a page. If you add or delete any text for example, text will be moved down the page to make way for the new text, or the gap will be filled up where some text was removed. Most d.t.p. programs permit graphics to be imported into documents, or you can reserve areas on pages which are left blank so that photographs or drawings can be pasted onto the printout. If areas are reserved before the text is imported, when the text is loaded it will automatically flow around the areas reserved for graphics. In effect you are creating "no-go" areas for the text.

With most d.t.p. programs it is possible to alter the sizes of graphics frames, and the text will again be adjusted to fit the new layout. Usually it is also possible to add graphics frames after the text has been loaded, with the text once more being reformatted to suit the altered page layout. If a graphics frame is moved, the text is automatically shuffled around to suit the frame's new position. This automatic reformatting, together with a WYSIWYG display, makes it easy to get page layouts looking right, and looking right at the first attempt. Repeatedly printing out pages, making alterations and reprinting them, is a very slow and costly method of working. With a good d.t.p. program you can produce page layouts quickly, and will need to undertake minimal reworking of documents.

With many d.t.p. programs you are restricted to having graphics in rectangular frames, with the text being kept off these areas altogether. Some d.t.p. programs have a slightly different approach, where the loaded drawing itself is the "no-go" area, rather than the frame into which it is loaded. This may seem to make no difference, but the point to keep in mind here is that a drawing might not fill the frame into which it is loaded. There may be blank areas of background, and quite large areas at that. If the text is repelled by the drawing rather than by the graphics frame, the text is free to flow into these blank areas in the background. The text will therefore flow around the outline of the drawing, giving what is quite a neat effect if it is used sensibly. Like many of the advanced facilities in d.t.p. programs, it is not a good idea to use it simply because it is there. Flowing text around drawings is not appropriate for many types of technical publication for example.

With d.t.p. programs which do not have a facility of this type it is sometimes possible to get much the same effect. First text is loaded into the frame, but the frame is not made a "no-go" area for the text. Several graphics frames are then created, and made "no-go" areas, so that they keep the text off the appropriate areas of the drawing. This is a less convenient way of handling things, but it gives more control over where the text goes. With some automatic flow-around facilities you might find that the text gets closer to the drawings than you would really like. You will often find that with d.t.p. programs there are indirect means of getting special effects even if there is no proper facility provided. It pays to read the manual carefully, and to give some thought to methods of using the available facilities.

It is perhaps worth mentioning that there are text frames as well as graphics frames. Like a graphics frame, a text type repels the main text and produces a blank area on the screen. Instead of loading a drawing into this area, it is loaded with a small piece of text. This may seem a bit pointless, but with some types of publication, particularly technical types, it is quite common to have these text boxes to carry detailed explanations of points raised in the main text. Without a text frame capability it could be quite difficult to handle these text boxes. Not all d.t.p. programs have this facility, but many can now handle this type of thing, although not necessarily in an entirely straightforward method.

Much d.t.p. work involves producing numerous documents that are all laid out very much along the same lines. In some cases it might be necessary to produce documents using several standard formats. Most up-market d.t.p. programs have some form of "style sheet" facility that enables the program to be tailored to suit one or more of these standard formats. The exact way in which this facility functions varies from program to program, but in most cases it is possible to produce finished documents largely automatically. With some embedded commands in the text file, and the right style sheet selected, the loaded text is given the right fonts and styles, flows into the required column format, and so on.

Obviously there will often be the need for some variation from one document to another, and it might not always be possible to produce finished documents without resorting to some manual editing. Using style sheets does not impede the program's editing facilities, so that any required customisation of documents can be carried out swiftly and easily.

Importing Graphics

Although most d.t.p. work is concerned with the manipulation of text, many documents also include some graphics. The easiest way to add graphics into a d.t.p. produced document is to simply reserve areas on the pages using the d.t.p. program, and to then print out the documents without the graphics. Next use the graphics program to print out the illustrations at the correct sizes, and paste them in place. This is a rather old fashioned way of handling things, but remember that it may not always be possible to load your illustrations into the d.t.p. program. Some d.t.p. programs are more accommodating than others in this respect. In general, programs that produce pixel type graphics are better supported than those that produce vector graphics. An advantage of the paste-up method is that it can be used with hand produced artwork and photographs.

It is important to realise that even if graphics can be imported into a d.t.p. program, which might require an indirect route, they might undergo unacceptable changes in the process. Exchanging graphics between programs is far more complex than text interchanges, particularly where vector graphics are involved. The paste-up method may be crude and old fashioned, but it can be applied using practically any d.t.p. and graphics software combination, and should ensure that very high quality results are obtained.

If you are lucky, your d.t.p. program will be able to directly import drawing files produced by your graphics program. Your chances of being able to do this are much better if the graphics program is a very popular type, or is one which can produce files that are in the same format as a popular graphics program. Assuming that the graphics program can produce drawings in a suitable file format, there should be no difficulty in loading the drawings into d.t.p. documents.

In some cases you might have the luxury of being able to produce drawing files in two or more formats that the d.t.p. program can read. If this should be the case it is probably worthwhile trying to load some typical illustrations in each of these formats. One format might be quicker and easier to use than the others, or it might give more faithful transfer of the drawings. With pixel based graphics it might not make any difference which format is used. Swapping pixel graphics between programs seems to be a relatively straightforward task. If problems should arise, such as changes in the aspect ratio of the drawing, these can often be overcome without too much difficulty. The aspect ratio of pixel graphics can often be adjusted in the d.t.p. program for instance.

With vector graphics there can be vast differences in the results obtained using different formats. In general, using a format that converts the vector graphics to a screen pixel format (such as an AutoCAD "slide" file) will give lower quality than one which transfers the drawing in vector graphic form. On the other hand, if the pixel format gives adequate results, this might be the quickest and most reliable method.

When transferring drawings in vector graphic form there are several potential problem areas. One of these is the text. If you have a drawing which has something like boxes containing nicely centred pieces of text, you might find that after the transfer the text is no longer centred properly. This type of thing seems to occur due to slight changes in the text size. In some cases the text grows so large that it goes well outside its normal limits, giving totally unusable results.

Another common problem area is line widths. These days most vector graphics programs are not restricted to a single line width. In fact most CAD and illustration programs permit you to use any line width you like. You may find that some file formats result in line width information being lost. This does not necessarily result in drawings being rendered totally useless after the transfer to the d.t.p. program, but there will clearly be an appreciable loss of quality.

You may find that the single line width used gives lines that are too fat, or that line width information is to some extent retained, but all the lines seem too wide. This type of thing can sometimes be corrected by altering the scaling or line widths in the drawing program. For example, halving all the line widths may give better results, as might drawing everything double size but leaving the line widths unaltered. If things do not go right first time, some experimentation will often result in more acceptable results.

In my experience the best vector graphics format to use when swapping drawings between two CAD programs, or a CAD program and a d.t.p. type, is the HPGL format. This is the language used to drive Hewlett Packard plotters, and HPGL simply stands for "Hewlett Packard Graphics Language". These plotters were very popular in the early days of computing, and as a result of this many plotter manufacturers have made their plotters HPGL compatible. This has led to virtually every vector graphics program having the ability to drive an HPGL plotter. The ability to output HPGL disk files is now a fairly standard feature, and some d.t.p. programs can read in these files.

The advantage of an HPGL file is that it results in no loss of information. The graphics program will have an HPGL driver which ensures that every object in the drawing is plotted out correctly, even if it is a very complex shape that has to be plotted as numerous very short lines. Even colour and layer information can be retained, since the HPGL format allows several different pens to be used. Different layers or colours can therefore be represented by different pens. As the HPGL format is not in any way tied to a particular type of computer, it is quite possible to swap these files between programs running on different computers.

Although the HPGL solution is in many ways an ideal one for swapping vector graphics, it does have a couple of minor drawbacks. One is that of pen widths. When plotting out drawings it is quite normal to use pens of various widths. Any program reading in an HPGL file will have no way of knowing what line width each pen should have. Even if only one pen is used, the program reading in the file might default to an incorrect width, or simply draw everything with the minimum line width. Ideally it should be possible to specify a line width for each pen, but this facility is usually absent. This problem can usually be overcome by using the drawing program's line width control to produce thick lines, rather than using notional thick pens. With a little experimentation it is usually possible to produce good results.

The second problem is simply that HPGL files can be quite large. Some programs produce more compact files than others. The HPGL includes commands to handle such things as arcs, circles, and text of various sizes, but many CAD programs produce everything using simple line plotting commands. This is to ensure that everything is plotted out exactly as it should be, with no changes in text size, text font, etc. With a large circle perhaps being plotted as a few hundred very short straight lines, obviously some very large files can be generated.

There should be no problem when using a computer that has reasonably high capacity disk drives and plenty of memory, but I suppose that the potential to overload the system is always there. The only certain way of discovering what you can and can not get away with is to try transferring some fairly complex drawings to see how the system copes with them. In some cases quite complex graphics can be accommodated, but it will take a long time for the files to be generated, and for them to be read into the d.t.p. program.

PostScript

PostScript is something that tends to be associated with the more up-market laser printers, and it is a page description language. It has similarities with the HPGL in that it can accommodate simple graphics shapes, etc., but it goes well beyond this. It can handle text in numerous fonts and sizes, complex fill patterns, and just about anything you would ever need to print out. PostScript is independent of the resolution of any particular device, and it will always make full use of the available resolution. Although in the past it has been mainly used as a means of sending page descriptions from d.t.p. or graphics programs to high quality printers, it actually has much wider applications. It can be used to exchange text and (or) graphics between two computer based devices, or between programs running on the same system.

The ability to produce PostScript files is now an increasingly common feature of graphics programs, especially those that can produce high resolution graphics, but it is still far from being a universal feature. Some d.t.p. programs have the ability to read-in PostScript files, but this is again a feature that is far from universal. I can not claim to have had much practical experience of this type of file exchange, and can not really comment on how well or otherwise it works in practice. Like the swapping of HPGL files, it seems to involve quite large files in many cases, which could cause problems. However, where everything in the system can handle this method of graphics interchange, it would seem to offer an excellent method of handling things. It should give a very faithful transfer of any illustration, with nothing being left out or lost in the transfer, and no loss of quality.

Terminology

Like just about any aspect of computing, with d.t.p. programs you are likely to encounter a number of terms which can be a bit confusing at first. One term you will certainly encounter, and one which has already cropped up a few times in this chapter, is "font". If you look through a few publications, you will notice that the shape of any selected letter varies somewhat from one publication to another. In fact it is not just the letters that are different. There are marked differences in the figures, and even the punctuation marks. Each set of character shapes is a text font. With most d.t.p. programs you will have a number of fonts available as standard, probably with a great many more available as optional extras.

It is important to differentiate between text fonts and styles. Each font can have a number of different styles. As a few examples, text can be in bold (heavy) print, in light print, in italics, or underlined. These are just variations on a given font, and do not count as new fonts. Virtually all d.t.p. programs permit a range of styles to be used, together with a wide range of text sizes. Even using just a couple of fonts, this permits a great deal of control to be exercised over the appearance of finished documents.

In Proportion

Two further terms you are likely to encounter are proportional spacing and kerning. These are similar, but definitely not different terms for the same thing. Proportional spacing is the more simple of the two. Obviously some letters take up more space than others. The letters "i" and "l" for example, are much thinner than the letters "W" and "M". With an ordinary typewriter or a computer printer used in its normal modes, this fact is ignored, and all letters are given the same amount of space. Thin characters appear well spaced out, and fat characters seem to be crammed together.

This is known as "monospacing", and d.t.p. programs do not normally work in this mode. Many d.t.p. programs do actually have the ability to use one or more monospaced fonts, but these are only used in a few special situations. They are sometimes required in technical and scientific publication work, and can be useful for tables and some types of list.

Desk top publishing programs normally operate on the basis of allocating each letter an amount of space which is in keeping with its width. This is proportional spacing, and it generally gives a much better appearance to the text.

Kerning takes proportional spacing a step further. Although you might think that the text would look as neat as possible with each letter given an amount of space which suits its width, in practice things are not quite this simple. Proportional spacing works well enough with letters that consist basically of vertical and horizontal lines, but it does not work so well with those that have sloping lines. In particular, there are problems when letters such as "A" and "V" are side-by-side. The gap between them tends to look too large.

In order to get the text to look absolutely right it is necessary to close up the gap slightly with letter combinations such as this. The amount that the gap needs to be closed up is to some extent a subjective matter, and I suppose that text which looks perfect to one person might not look quite right to someone else. In general, the larger the text size, the more the text will need to be closed up on letter combinations of this type.

This closing up of the text is kerning. Most d.t.p. programs will automatically adjust the positions of letters so as to give a neater appearance to the text, and this is automatic kerning. As already pointed out, kerning is to some extent a subjective matter, and you might not always agree with the way in which the program kerns some of the text. There is often a facility that enables the positions of the text characters to be adjusted manually (manual kerning), so that the text can be "fine tuned" to what you subjectively judge to be perfection.

Going through pages of text adjusting the positions of hundreds of characters manually would be a very time consuming process, and manual kerning is not normally used in 'this way. It is mainly reserved for use where the program seems to have done things very badly, and for adjusting large text in headings and sub-headings. It is in small pieces of large sized text that any slight ineptitude in the kerning will be most apparent, and where careful manual kerning is most likely to be needed.

You will normally have the choice of justified or unjustified text. Most publications and documents are printed using justified text where this option is available, as it gives a neater and more professional appearance to the finished product. The main exception is where several narrow columns are used. Justified text can then result in large numbers of inserted spaces, and what are often rather scrappy looking results.

Sometimes the justification is controlled by having "switches" to control left- and right-hand justification. Left-hand justification is then what would normally be considered unjustified text. Right-hand justification only, gives a special effect where the right-hand margin is neat and the left-hand margin is ragged.

Normally where a long word is too long to fit into the space at the end of a line, it is placed on the subsequent line. If justification is used, this can result in a large number of spaces being added to pad out the line into which the word would not fit. This can give scrappy looking results. To avoid this, hyphenation is often used. This is where the word is split into two sections, with the first part at the end of one line, and the rest of the word on the subsequent line. A hyphen is used at the end of the first section of the word. Most publications that are printed with justified text are also hyphenated (including this one).

Desk top publishing programs mostly have an automatic hyphenation facility, but this may not always operate in a satisfactory way. Most automatic hyphenation systems are reasonably efficient, but few are guaranteed not to make even the occasional blunder. With the word "hyphenation" for instance, it might be hyphenated in the form "hyphe-nation", whereas most people would probably deem "hyphen-ation" or even "hyph-enation" to be better alternatives. Where the automatic hyphenation does not give the desired result, there should be no difficulty in doing some manual editing in order to sort things out.

Some rather quaint types of measurement are used in the printing industry, and when using a d.t.p. program you are almost certain to encounter one or two of these. The one you are most likely to come across is point size, which is mainly used as a means of selecting the required text size. Point sizes are in 1/72s of an inch, and simply dividing a point figure by 72 gives the height of capital letters in inches. Multiplying a point size by 0.353 gives the size in millimetres.

You may also encounter ems. An em is not a fixed size, and one em is equivalent to the point size of the font in use. It is mainly used when setting the spacing between words, and by having it related to the font size, it will automatically give lesser or greater spacing on smaller and larger character sizes (respectively). Ems are also used for other purposes, such as specifying the spacing between lines and paragraphs. Again, this has the advantage of giving greater spacing on larger text sizes, although you may be able to independently control the line and paragraph spacing at various points in a document should you wish to do so. Note that d.t.p. programs do not necessarily operate on the basis of simple single line spacing, double line spacing, etc. They mostly give much finer control than this. The gap between lines of text is known as the "leading" distance incidentally.

In Practice

Having considered d.t.p. in general, we will now consider how things are done using Timeworks in particular. We can only consider the basic way in which the program is used, as there is insufficient space available for a detailed discussion of this program's many features. However, for present purposes a general run-down on how the program is used should suffice.

The first task is to either load a style sheet which sets up the program with the desired page size, column layout, etc., or you must design everything from scratch. Here we will assume that the starting from scratch approach is to be used. If the "New" option is selected from the "File" menu, you are asked via a pop-up "dialogue box" if you wish to load a style sheet. If you answer no to this question, the control panel of Figure 3.4 appears on the screen. This allows you to select the desired page size and orientation.

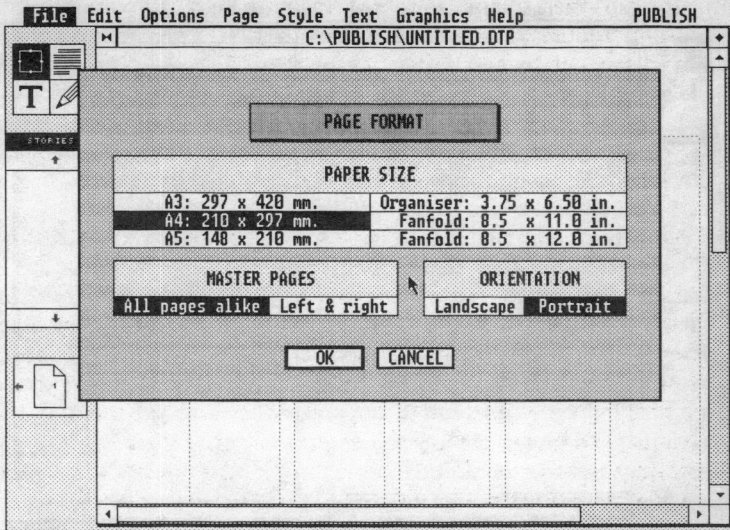

```
 File  Edit  Options  Page  Style  Text  Graphics  Help         PUBLISH
┌──────────────────────────────────────────────────────────────────────┐
│ ⊠                    C:\PUBLISH\UNTITLED.DTP                      ◆  │
│ ┌─┐ ▤                                                            ▲  │
│ └─┘                                                                 │
│ T ✎                                                                 │
│                                                                     │
│ STORIES                                                             │
│   ↑   ┌──────────────────────────────────────────────────────┐     │
│       │          ┌───────────────────────────┐               │     │
│       │          │        PAGE FORMAT         │               │     │
│       │          └───────────────────────────┘               │     │
│       │                                                       │     │
│       │                    PAPER SIZE                         │     │
│       │   ┌───────────────────────────────────────────────┐  │     │
│       │   │ A3: 297 x 420 mm.  │ Organiser: 3.75 x 6.50 in.│  │     │
│       │   │ A4: 210 x 297 mm.  │   Fanfold: 8.5  x 11.0 in.│  │     │
│   ↓   │   │ A5: 148 x 210 mm.  │   Fanfold: 8.5  x 12.0 in.│  │     │
│       │   └───────────────────────────────────────────────┘  │     │
│       │   ┌──────────────────────┐ ▸ ┌──────────────────────┐│     │
│ ┌───┐ │   │     MASTER PAGES     │   │     ORIENTATION      ││     │
│ │ 1 │ │   │ All pages alike│Left & right│ Landscape│Portrait ││     │
│ └───┘ │   └──────────────────────┘   └──────────────────────┘│     │
│ ↤     │              ┌──────┐   ┌────────┐                    │     │
│       │              │  OK  │   │ CANCEL │                    │     │
│       │              └──────┘   └────────┘                    │     │
│       └──────────────────────────────────────────────────────┘     │
│                                                                  ▼  │
│ ◄                                                             ►     │
└──────────────────────────────────────────────────────────────────────┘
```

Fig. 3.4   The control panel used to select the required page size and
orientation

Having selected the required options from this control panel,
the mouse/pointer are "clicked" on the "OK" box, and you are
then back in the main screen (Fig. 3.5).   Timeworks is largely
controlled via a menu bar and pop-down menus, or via keyboard
codes if preferred.   It does make use of icons in a limited way
though, and four of them can be seen towards the top left-hand
corner of the screen.   These are used to place the program in the
appropriate operating mode for the type of task you wish to
undertake.   Starting in the top left-hand corner and working in a
clockwise direction, the icons give access to the frame, paragraph,
graphics, and text modes.

Initially it is the frame mode that is required, and this is the
one that is selected in Figure 3.5 (hence the frame icon is shown
in inverse video).   In this mode you draw boxes into which the
text and (or) graphics will be placed.   In this example there are
three frames: one at the top which is the full page width and is
designed to take a large heading, and two beneath this which

83

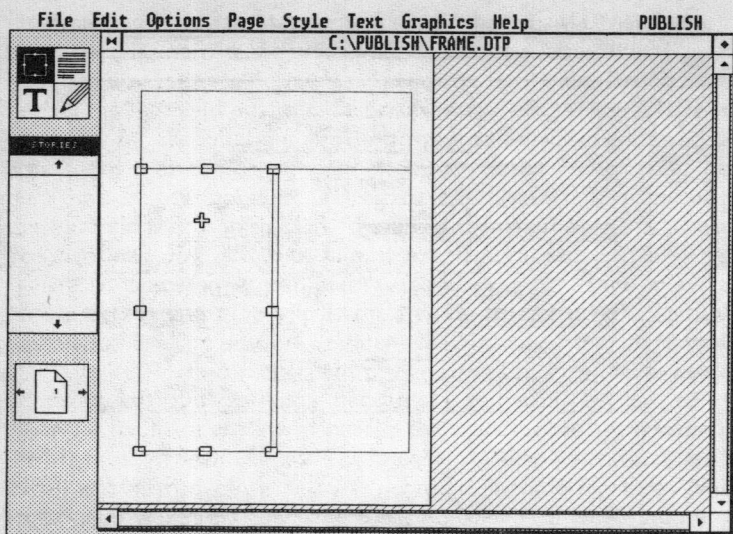

Fig. 3.5   The main screen with the frame mode selected. Three frames have been drawn on the page, and the bottom left-hand frame is the current one

give two columns of normal text. There are on-screen guide marks to help you get things right (these are hidden beneath the frames in Figure 3.5), and optional rulers can be switched on as further aids to getting the frame sizes right.

Note though, that it is by no means essential to get this right first time. The frame sizes can be adjusted at this stage, or later when they are occupied. "Clicking" the mouse in a frame selects it as the current one, and eight "handles" (the small squares visible on one frame in Figure 3.5) then appear. These enable the frame to be altered in size. Simply placing the on-screen pointer in a frame and then holding down the mouse button enables the frame to be dragged around the screen. The text is automatically adjusted to fit into the frames properly, with pieces of text being moved from one frame to another if a change in frame size should make this necessary.

In order to load the text the appropriate option is chosen from the "File" menu, and the required text file is then selected using the control panel that appears on screen. Note that you can load several text files if necessary, and a list of the files that are loaded appears in the panel beneath the four mode icons. At this stage no text flows into the frames. In order to put text in a frame you must first select the frame by "clicking" on it, and then select the text file from the list of files using the same method. By selecting the appropriate frames and files you can load any piece of text into any frame. Where text is spread across several frames, the program will automatically split the text between frames in the most efficient manner. All you have to do is make sure that you select the frames in the right order!

So far we have not mentioned graphics, but these can be loaded into the program and placed in frames in much the same way as text. There are separate on-screen lists for text, pixel, and vector graphics files, and it is easy to move from one list to the next using a "click" of the mouse. Of course, with graphics the complete drawing always goes into one frame, however big or small that frame happens to be, and it will not be split between frames. Figure 3.6 shows a drawing loaded into a frame. This cartoon was produced using Deluxe Paint II Enhanced, saved in "PCX" format, and then loaded into Timeworks.

Having loaded the text into the program, it must then be formatted correctly. This is done first of all using the paragraph mode. When this mode is selected, the panel on the left-hand side of the screen shows a list of the available text sizes (refer back to Figure 3.3). Initially everything is in the default "body text" size, font, and style. In order to change a piece of text to a different font/text size, first the mouse is "clicked" on the appropriate paragraph, and it is then shown in inverse video so that you know exactly what text you are operating on. Again, this is shown in Figure 3.3. "Clicking" the mouse on a different type of text in the list then results in the paragraph being changed to this new type of text. A number of different default text types are available, but you are free to modify these or set up your own from scratch.

Although this mode is called the "paragraph" mode, what it is actually operating on is the piece of text between two carriage returns. Consequently, it can be used to pick out and change

Fig. 3.6   A drawing produced using Deluxe Paint II Enhanced loaded into Timeworks

headings and sub-headings just as easily as it can be used to alter paragraphs. In fact the normal way of using the program is to have the body text set up as the text font, style, and size that you need for the main text. The headings and sub-headings are then picked out and altered to larger text, probably in a different font and style as well. This keeps the amount of formatting needed to an absolute minimum.

In the text mode the program has a cursor that is much the same as the cursor of a word processor program. It enables the text to be altered on a letter-by-letter basis, for making spelling corrections and small formatting changes. The graphics mode gives access to some simple drawing commands, but in common with most other d.t.p. programs, we are talking here in terms of some very basic capabilities. Most graphics have to be drawn up in a separate program and imported into Timeworks.

The pop-down menus add to and considerably enhance the main editing features of the program, and provide a considerable

86

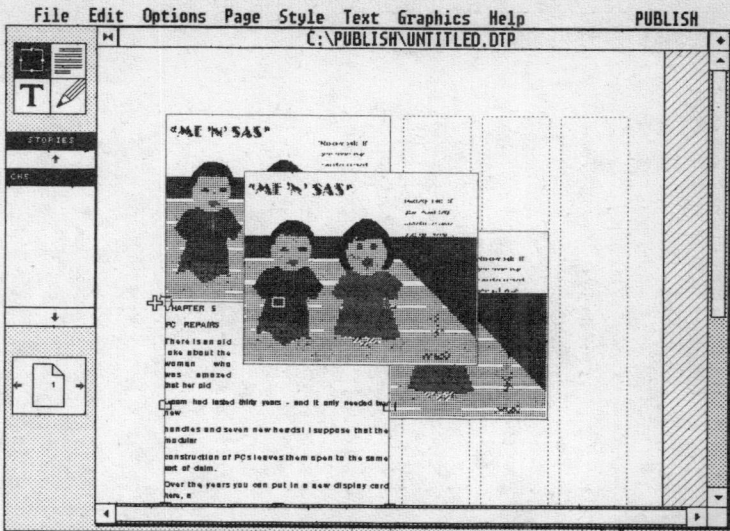

Fig. 3.7 Frames can be "stacked" in order to give special effects

degree of control over the final documents. The "view" menu for example, provides pan and zoom facilities, but it also enables pages to be added, deleted, or inserted into the document. It also provides a simple special effect which enables one frame to partially cover and obscure another frame (rather like Corel Draw!'s ability to stack objects one on top of the other). A simple (and rather inept) example of this is shown in Figure 3.7. With a program like Timeworks there are plenty of "tricks" available if you want them.

Chapter 4

DATABASES, SPREADSHEETS AND UTILITIES, ETC.

A database is simply a store of information, which should really be arranged in a logical fashion in order to fully qualify as a database. Databases were in existence long before micro-computers came into existence. A filing cabinet full of invoices and a card index are both examples of databases. A computer running a database program provides much the same facilities as a card index, but it has some tremendous advantages. One of these is the speed with which the required records can be sorted out from what could well be hundreds or even thousands of entries. Databases have search facilities that make it easy to seek out the required records. This factor has led to them almost totally replacing card indexes, etc., in most businesses.

Some database programs are designed specifically for one task, while others are adaptable for operation in just about any database application. There is an advantage of the single use type in that they are fully set up and ready to go, or something close to it, and you merely have to feed in the data before they are ready for use. They obviously have a serious drawback in that they lack versatility, and if you need several databases, with this type of program you will need a different program for each set of data.

The adaptable type may take a little longer in the initial setting up stage, and may require a little more expertise on the part of the user, but they have the advantage of fulfilling all your database requirements. If you need two or three dozen sets of data, then a single adaptable database program should be able to handle all these without any difficulty. In most cases there is no real choice but to use an adaptable database, since suitable custom database programs are simply not available. Here we will only consider adaptable database programs.

dBASE IV
The dBASE series of programs are almost certainly the most popular database programs at present. Probably the best way to

```
    Data        Queries      Forms      Reports     Labels    Applications
 ┌──────────┐┌──────────┐┌──────────┐┌──────────┐┌──────────┐┌──────────┐
 │ <create> ││ <create> ││ <create> ││ <create> ││ <create> ││ <create> │
 │ INDEX1   ││          ││          ││          ││          ││          │
 │          ││          ││          ││          ││          ││          │
 │          ││          ││          ││          ││          ││          │
 │          ││          ││          ││          ││          ││          │
 └──────────┘└──────────┘└──────────┘└──────────┘└──────────┘└──────────┘

 File:          New file
 Description:   Press ENTER on <create> to create a new file


 Help:F1  Use:◄┘  Data:F2  Design:Shift-F2  Quick Report:Shift-F9  Menus:F10
```

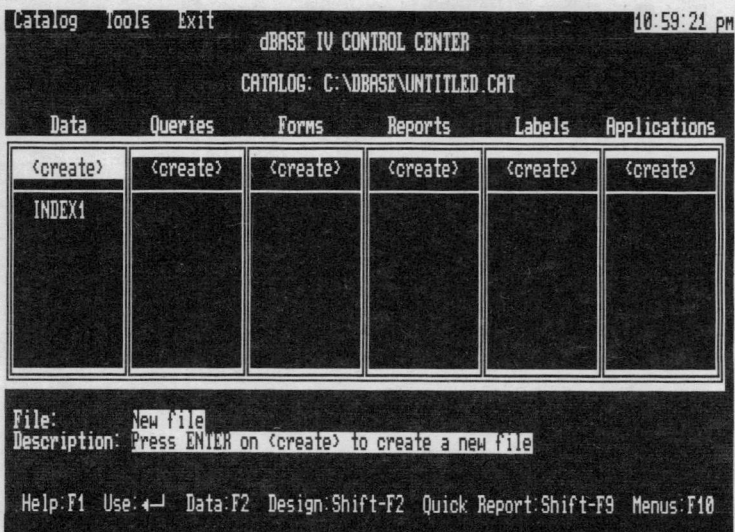

Fig. 4.1   The dBASE IV control centre

explain the basics of database programs is to jump straight in
and look at the way in which dBASE is used. Note that the
description which follows is based on dBASE IV, and that earlier
versions of dBASE are not controlled in quite the same manner.
In particular, they do not have the control centre. When you
first run dBASE IV the main control centre display appears on
the screen, as shown in the screen dump of Figure 4.1. Across
the middle of the screen there are six headings ("Data",
"Queries", etc.) which provide access to the main functions of
the program. Below each heading there is the word "create",
and beneath this there are lists of disk files. On the example
screen there is actually only one file listed ("INDEX1" under the
"Data" heading), since the program is only in the initial stages of
being set up. When the program is first run there are no files
listed at all, since you will obviously not have created any at that
stage.

The selected file or "create" option is shown highlighted in
inverse video. The cursor controls are used to select different

options by moving the highlighted block around, and pressing the "Return" key actually takes you into the selected option. You will notice there is also a conventional menu bar at the top left-hand section of the screen, and this gives access to three pop-down menus. A pop-down menu can be activated by pressing the "Alt" key and then the first letter of the menu name (e.g. "Alt" and "C" to select the "Catalog" menu). Additionally, some keyboard codes are listed at the bottom of the screen, and these provide a means of accessing some functions of the program. For example, pressing the "F2" key takes the program into the "Data" mode, which enables you to browse through the data in the loaded database.

With many database programs (including earlier versions of dBASE) cataloguing of files is not essential. It is compulsory with dBASE IV though, since files will only appear in the control centre file lists if they are in the current catalogue. This means that they are not accessible unless they are catalogued. Each catalogue normally contains files of a similar type that you might wish to use together. Different catalogues are used for different applications of the program. This helps to keep things well organised with the different applications kept well and truly separated. Apart from making the program easier to use, this should avoid accidentally loading an incorrect file and possibly modifying it before the mistake is spotted.

By default a catalogue called "UNTITLED.CAT" is used, but normally this would be changed by first selecting the "Catalog" menu. Then the "Use A Different Catalog" option is selected, followed by the "Create" option from the sub-menu that appears. After the new catalogue name has been typed in and the "Return" key has been pressed, you are taken back to the control centre once again. You are then ready to start creating the database.

The normal starting point is to select the "Create" option under the "Data" heading. At this stage you will not actually be putting data into the program — you must first set up the program with suitable fields. With a card index you must decide what information you are going to put on each card, and in what order the various pieces of information will appear. Each piece of information goes into the appropriate area of the card, or into its particular "field". The situation is similar with an

91

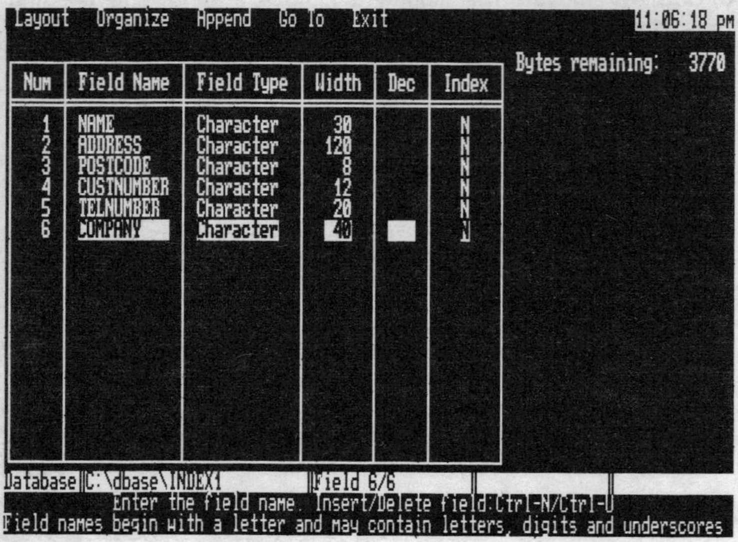

```
Layout  Organize  Append  Go To  Exit                    11:06:18 PM
                                          Bytes remaining:     3770

┌─────┬────────────┬────────────┬───────┬─────┬────────┐
│ Num │ Field Name │ Field Type │ Width │ Dec │ Index  │
├─────┼────────────┼────────────┼───────┼─────┼────────┤
│  1  │ NAME       │ Character  │   30  │     │   N    │
│  2  │ ADDRESS    │ Character  │  120  │     │   N    │
│  3  │ POSTCODE   │ Character  │    8  │     │   N    │
│  4  │ CUSTNUMBER │ Character  │   12  │     │   N    │
│  5  │ TELNUMBER  │ Character  │   20  │     │   N    │
│  6  │ COMPANY    │ Character  │   40  │     │   N    │
└─────┴────────────┴────────────┴───────┴─────┴────────┘

Database C:\dbase\INDEX1        Field 6/6
        Enter the field name. Insert/Delete field:Ctrl-N/Ctrl-U
Field names begin with a letter and may contain letters, digits and underscores
```

Fig. 4.2   Setting up the fields for a database

electronic database, and Figure 4.2 shows an example set of
fields.

When setting up the fields for a database it is generally better
to split the information across several fields rather than put
everything into just one or two fields. This leaves your options
open, and generally makes things easier when searching for
entries, etc. When setting up a database it is a good idea to
create a likely looking set of fields, put in a few database entries,
and then try using this mini-database. Any mistakes in the
arrangement you have used will soon come to light, and from
the experience you gain with the mini-database it is easy to go
back and set up an improved version. You will have taken up
little time in doing this, which will not be the case if you create
a set of fields, add thousands of entries, and then find that it is
difficult or impossible to use properly!

When generating a set of fields you must specify a name for
each field, and this makes life easier when adding entries into
the database. The field names appear on the screen when you

```
 Records      Go To    Exit                              11:04:35 pm
NAME          Fred Bloggs,
ADDRESS       123 The Street, Atown, Adistrict, Acounty.

POSTCODE      AB1 2YZ
CUSTNUMBER    123456789
TELNUMBER     071 1234 123456
COMPANY       Widget Industries Ltd.




Edit    C:\dbase\INDEX1        Rec 1/1         File
```

Fig. 4.3   An example entry based on the fields shown in Figure 4.2

add entries to the database (Fig. 4.3), or when you examine
entries at some later time. This makes it easy to add information
in the right fields when creating or editing entries, and to inter-
pret the data when extracting information from entries. The
type of field must also be specified, but here we will only consider character types. This is the default type, and is simply
one that contains text characters (including figures, and punctuation marks). The field width must also be given, and this is
simply the maximum number of characters (including spaces,
etc.) that will need to appear in a field. Obviously you must be
careful to make the fields large enough, but making them un-
necessarily large will simply make life difficult when browsing
through the database. You will be faced with largely empty
screens, making it difficult to find the data you require.

The "Dec" entry is the number of decimal places, but this
only applies to numeric fields, not to character types. Although
you might think that the telephone and customer numbers
should be numeric fields, this is not the case. In dBASE a

numeric field is a numeric value, such as a price or the number of runs scored by a batsman in a cricket match. In other words, a piece of data which you might wish to mathematically manipulate in some way. Neither the customer numbers nor the telephone numbers are in this category.

Last and by no means least, there is the option of indexing a field. The two main ways in which databases are used are to search for specific pieces of information in a field, and to sort fields into a particular order (alpha-numeric, date order, or whatever). Indexing is related to the sorting of fields. The basic idea is for the program to produce a file that gives the correct order for sorted entries. The database entries are not actually sorted into the correct order at this stage, but with the aid of the index file they can be quickly sorted if necessary. Sorting is crucial to some database applications, but with many it is only the ability to seek out entries that meet certain criteria that is required.

In the data mode there is a very useful browse facility which enables you to view all the entries in a database. This shows each entry on a single line, which often means that the entries will be too wide to fit the screen. A system of sideways scrolling (Figs 4.4 and 4.5) enables all the fields to be viewed even if they occupy more than the 80-character width of the screen, but obviously only some of the fields can be viewed at any one time. Normally there will be more entries than a single screenful can accommodate, but the normal system of vertical scrolling enables an almost limitless number of entries to be accommodated. A drop-down menu provides facilities that make it easier to navigate your way around large databases. Note that the drop-down menus that are available is something which varies as the program is switched between its various operating modes. Although there are usually only three or four header words in the menu bar, there are numerous sets of header words, and dozens of different menus.

Sorting

A typical example of sorting is where a database must be sorted into alphabetical order, based on names, addresses, postcodes, or whatever. The data can be sorted using any field as the basis of the sorting operation, so having the data split up into a number

```
NAME                        ADDRESS
Mr.J.Smith                  57 The Street, London
Fred Bloggs                 123 The Street, Atown, Adistrict, Acounty
Mr.H.I.Jump                 65 The Avenue, Avillage, Somewhere
Mr.I.M.Perfect              12 Wonerful Street, Perfectville, Perfectshire
Mr.D.Base                   54 Feild Road, Recordtown, Essex
Mr.Dai Ode                  1 Way Street, Circuitous, Sussex
Mr.Mike Rochip              56 Silicon Street, Silicon Glen
Mr.Mike Roprocessor         65 Silicon Street, Silicon Glen
Miss L.E.Phant              76 Jungle Street, Wallow, Somerset
Ms.N.E.Time                 12 Clock Street, Timeout, W.Yorks.
Mr.N.E.Plaice               45 Haddock Street, Codsworth, Lancs
Mrs.N.E.Wear                23 Somewhere Road, Ware, Herts.
Mr.C.D.Hotel                123 High Street, Sometown, Sussex
Mr.R.D.Annual               65 Sunflower Road, Petal, Cornwall
Mrs.X.E.Lent                67 Wonderful Road, Hadford, Kent
Miss Tanya Bottom           2 Lowfield Avenue, Boxford, Surrey
Mrs.Nora Bone               23 Dog Road, Kennelworth, Bucks.
```

```
Browse  C:\dbase\INDEX1      Rec 1/17       File
                    View and edit fields
```

Fig. 4.4   The browse mode showing the first two fields

of fields keeps your options open, and enables the data to be sorted in practically any manner you like. In order to sort the data the "Shift" and "F2" keys are pressed, which brings up the "design" screen, and brings down the "Organize" menu. The "Create New Index" option is selected, and the new index is given a suitable name (Fig. 4.6). You then select the field on which the sorting must be based, and whether the sorting should be in ascending or descending order.

Having set up the required parameters, pressing the "Control" and "End" keys results in the index being produced. By entering the browse screen you can then examine the sorted database. Figures 4.7 and 4.8 respectively show the example database after it has been sorted in ascending order on the postcode field, and descending order on the customer number field.

Queries
Much database work involves locating entries that meet certain criteria. For example, you might wish to pick out the entry for

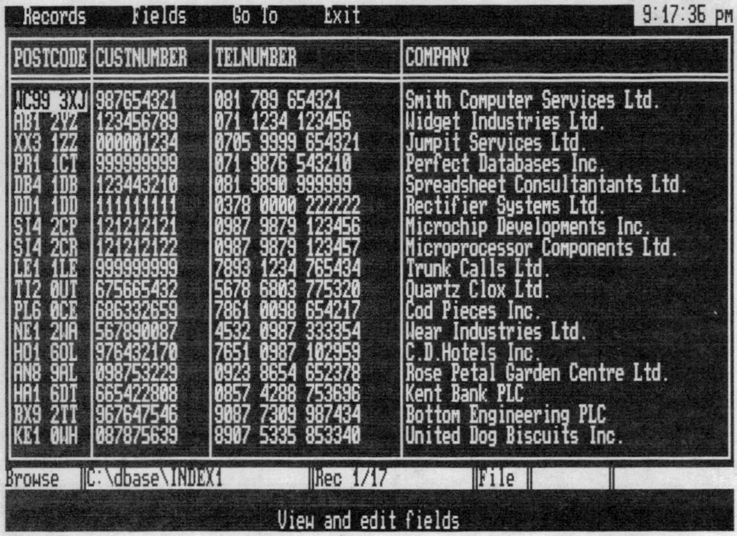

```
┌─────────────────────────────────────────────────────────────────────────────┐
│ Records     Fields    Go To    Exit                           9:17:36 pm     │
├──────────┬───────────┬──────────────────┬───────────────────────────────────┤
│ POSTCODE │CUSTNUMBER │ TELNUMBER        │ COMPANY                           │
├──────────┼───────────┼──────────────────┼───────────────────────────────────┤
│ NC99 3XJ │987654321  │081 789 654321    │ Smith Computer Services Ltd.      │
│ AB1 2YZ  │123456789  │071 1234 123456   │ Widget Industries Ltd.            │
│ XX3 1ZZ  │000001234  │0705 9999 654321  │ Jumpit Services Ltd.              │
│ PR1 1CT  │999999999  │071 9876 543210   │ Perfect Databases Inc.            │
│ DB4 1DB  │123443210  │081 9890 999999   │ Spreadsheet Consultantants Ltd.   │
│ DD1 1DD  │111111111  │0378 0000 222222  │ Rectifier Systems Ltd.            │
│ SI4 2CP  │121212121  │0987 9879 123456  │ Microchip Developments Inc.       │
│ SI4 2CR  │121212122  │0987 9879 123457  │ Microprocessor Components Ltd.    │
│ LE1 1LE  │999999999  │7893 1234 765434  │ Trunk Calls Ltd.                  │
│ TI2 0UT  │675665432  │5678 6803 775320  │ Quartz Clox Ltd.                  │
│ PL6 0CE  │686332659  │7861 0098 654217  │ Cod Pieces Inc.                   │
│ NE1 2WR  │567890087  │4532 0987 333354  │ Wear Industries Ltd.              │
│ HO1 60L  │976432170  │7651 0987 102959  │ C.D.Hotels Inc.                   │
│ AN8 9AL  │098753229  │0923 8654 652378  │ Rose Petal Garden Centre Ltd.     │
│ HA1 6DT  │665422808  │0857 4288 753696  │ Kent Bank PLC                     │
│ BX9 2TT  │967647546  │9087 7309 987434  │ Bottom Engineering PLC            │
│ KE1 0WH  │087875639  │8907 5335 853340  │ United Dog Biscuits Inc.          │
├──────────┴───────────┴──────────────────┴───────────────────────────────────┤
│ Browse  ║C:\dbase\INDEX1     ║Rec 1/17      ║File ║                           │
├─────────────────────────────────────────────────────────────────────────────┤
│                           View and edit fields                                │
└─────────────────────────────────────────────────────────────────────────────┘
```

Fig. 4.5   Sideways scrolling shows the remaining fields

a particular name, or perhaps you only have a customer number and no name to go on. In either case it would be possible to sort the database, and then quickly work through it until you located the right entry. However, with this type of thing it is generally much quicker and easier to get the database to locate the entry with the appropriate name, customer number, or whatever. This is done using the "Queries" mode of dBASE IV.

This is the second option available from the control centre. Selecting this takes you into the query design screen (Fig. 4.9). This screen is divided into two sections. At the bottom of the screen there are the fields in the database, and you use this section of the screen to select the fields that you wish to be displayed. Incidentally, the default is for all the fields to be displayed, and this will often be perfectly satisfactory. If there is insufficient screen space to permit all the fields to be shown on a single screenful, then the system of sideways scrolling comes into operation so that all the fields can be accommodated.

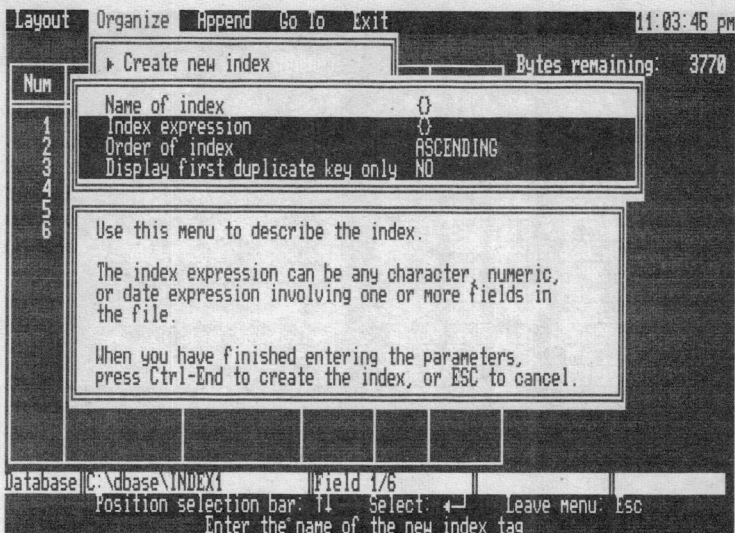

```
Layout  Organize  Append  Go To  Exit                11:03:46 pm
       ┌─► Create new index ──────────────────┐  Bytes remaining:  3770
┌─────┐│                                      │
│ Num │├──────────────────────────────────────┤
│     ││ Name of index                  {}     │
│ 1   ││ Index expression               {}     │
│ 2   ││ Order of index                 ASCENDING
│ 3   ││ Display first duplicate key only NO   │
│ 4   │└──────────────────────────────────────┘
│ 5   │┌──────────────────────────────────────┐
│ 6   ││ Use this menu to describe the index.  │
│     ││                                       │
│     ││ The index expression can be any character, numeric,
│     ││ or date expression involving one or more fields in
│     ││ the file.                             │
│     ││                                       │
│     ││ When you have finished entering the parameters,
│     ││ press Ctrl-End to create the index, or ESC to cancel.
│     │└──────────────────────────────────────┘
├─────┴─────────────────────────────────────────────────┐
│Database│C:\dbase\INDEX1      │Field 1/6                 │
        Position selection bar: ↑↓   Select: ◄┘   Leave menu: Esc
                 Enter the name of the new index tag
```

Fig. 4.6   Creating an index to sort the database

The top part of the screen is used to specify the conditions
that must be met by an entry in order for it to appear in the
filtered version of the database. There are a variety of mathematical and logical operators that can be used here, but in many
cases you will simply want to specify a string of characters (a
name, postcode, etc.), and have the program search for an entry
that matches that string in the appropriate field. The string of
characters must be placed in double quotation marks.

You can have a condition in just one field, or in several, as
required. A match will only be produced if all conditions are
met. If more than one entry produces a match, then all the
appropriate entries will be passed through to the filtered version
of the database. In the example of Figure 4.9 the only condition
is the name "Mr C. D. Hotel" in the "Name" field, and this
produces only a single match with the example database (Fig.
4.10).

There are numerous refinements to the query system, and one
of these is the ability to use "wildcards". In other words, rather

POSTCODE	CUSTNUMBER	TELNUMBER	COMPANY
AB1 2YZ	123456789	071 1234 123456	Widget Industries Ltd.
AN8 9AL	098753229	0923 8654 652378	Rose Petal Garden Centre Ltd.
BX9 2TT	962647546	9087 7309 987434	Bottom Engineering PLC
DB4 1DB	123443210	081 9890 999999	Spreadsheet Consultantants Ltd.
DD1 1DD	111111111	0378 0000 222222	Rectifier Systems Ltd.
HA1 6DT	665422808	0857 4288 753696	Kent Bank PLC
HO1 6OL	976432170	7651 0987 102959	C.D.Hotels Inc.
KE1 0WH	087875639	8907 5335 853340	United Dog Biscuits Inc.
LE1 1LE	999999999	7893 1234 765434	Trunk Calls Ltd.
NE1 2WA	567890087	4532 0987 333354	Wear Industries Ltd.
PL6 0CE	686332659	7861 0098 654217	Cod Pieces Inc.
PR1 1CT	999999999	071 9876 543210	Perfect Databases Inc.
SI4 2CP	121212121	0987 9879 123456	Microchip Developments Inc.
SI4 2CR	121212122	0987 9879 123457	Microprocessor Components Ltd.
TI2 0UT	675665432	5678 6803 775320	Quartz Clox Ltd.
WC99 3XJ	987654321	081 789 654321	Smith Computer Services Ltd.
XX3 1ZZ	000001234	0705 9999 654321	Jumpit Services Ltd.

Browse   C:\dbase\INDEX1   Rec 2/17   File

View and edit fields

Fig. 4.7   The example database sorted in ascending order on the postcode field

than specifying every character in a string, you can use a question mark (?) in the place of one or more characters. For instance, if you were not sure if a name was spelt "Hogwash" or "Hogwish", using "Hogw?sh" as the filter would provide a match in either case. There is an interesting "Sounds Like" facility, which will provide a match if the specified string sounds like a string found in the appropriate field of an entry. Again, this is something that could be useful if you are not sure of the correct spelling of a name. It does not seem to work quite as well as some of the word processor spelling checkers which have a similar phonetic checking mode, but it is nevertheless a very powerful and useful feature.

Labels
Apparently many people buy dBASE and then only use it to print out address labels. This is a task that the program can handle very well, but it's a bit like buying a double-decker bus to

POSTCODE	CUSTNUMBER	TELNUMBER	COMPANY
LE1 1LE	999999999	7893 1234 765434	Trunk Calls Ltd.
PR1 1CT	999999998	071 9876 543210	Perfect Databases Inc.
WC99 3XJ	987654321	081 789 654321	Smith Computer Services Ltd.
HO1 6OL	976432170	7651 0987 102959	C.D.Hotels Inc.
BX9 2TT	967647546	9087 7309 987434	Bottom Engineering PLC
PL6 0CE	686332659	7861 0098 654217	Cod Pieces Inc.
TI2 0UT	675665432	5678 6803 775320	Quartz Clox Ltd.
HA1 6DT	665422808	0857 4288 753696	Kent Bank PLC
NE1 2WA	567890087	4532 0987 333354	Wear Industries Ltd.
AB1 2YZ	123456789	071 1234 123456	Widget Industries Ltd.
DB4 1DB	123443210	081 9890 999999	Spreadsheet Consultantants Ltd.
SI4 2CR	121212122	0987 9879 123457	Microprocessor Components Ltd.
SI4 2CP	121212121	0987 9879 123456	Microchip Developments Inc.
DD1 1DD	111111111	0378 0000 222222	Rectifier Systems Ltd.
AN8 9AL	098753229	0923 8654 652378	Rose Petal Garden Centre Ltd.
KE1 0WH	087875639	8907 5335 853340	United Dog Biscuits Inc.
XX3 1ZZ	000001234	0705 9999 654321	Jumpit Services Ltd.

```
Browse  |C:\dbase\INDEX1      |Rec 9/17      |File |        |
                        View and edit fields
```

Fig. 4.8   In this case the database has been sorted on the
"CUSTNUMBER" field in descending order

get you to and from work. There are label printing programs
that will handle this job perfectly well if you do not need any
of the other facilities of dBASE IV.

The label mode is selected from the control centre, and you
are then placed into the label design screen (Fig. 4.11). You
have a number of options when designing labels, and the
"Dimensions" menu for instance, gives access to options that
enable the width and height of the label to be altered, together
with controls governing factors such as line spacing and the
number of columns in which the labels should be printed (Fig.
4.12).

Having setup a label of the required dimensions, etc., or having
simply accepted the default settings, the next task is to place the
fields on the label. To do this you simply place the cursor (a
flashing square within the label area) where you want the first
character of the field to appear. Pressing the "F5" key then
brings down the "Fields" menu, and you can select the desired

```
 Layout  Fields  Condition  Update  Exit                    9:57:28 PM
┌──────────────────────────────────────────────────────────────────────┐
│ Index1.dbf │ ↓NAME            │ ↓ADDRESS         │ ↓POSTCODE           │
├────────────┴──────────────────┴──────────────────┴─────────────────────┤
│             "Mr.C.D.Hotel"                                              │
│                                                                         │
│                                                                         │
│                                                                         │
│                                                                         │
│                                                                         │
│  View                                                                   │
│  <NEW>       Index1->        Index1->         Index1->      Index1->    │
│              NAME            ADDRESS          POSTCODE      CUSTNUMBER   │
│                                                                         │
└─────────────────────────────────────────────────────────────────────────┘
 Query   C:\dbase\<NEW>          Field 1/6
  Prev/Next field:Shift-Tab/Tab  Data:F2  Pick:Shift-F1  Prev/Next skel:F3/F4
```

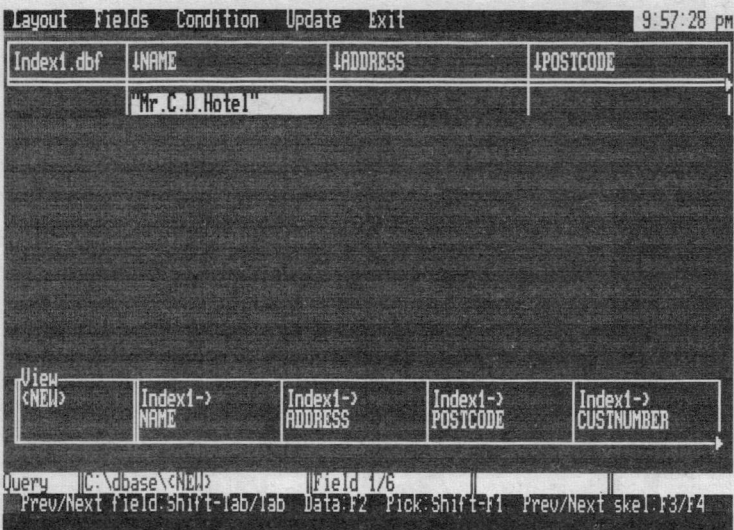

Fig. 4.9   The query design screen

field (Fig. 4.13). Apart from the fields you have generated yourself, there are some standard ones such as the time and the date,
plus (where appropriate) calculated fields. Having positioned and
selected the fields you require, you end up with a "dummy" label
displayed in the centre of the screen. This has rows of Xs to
represent the lines of text in an actual label, as in Figure 4.14.
The number of Xs is equal to the maximum number of characters
for each field. If there is insufficient space available for a complete field, the program will simply truncate it.

Finally, having fully set up the required label format, the
"Print" option can be selected, and the labels can be printed out.
As usual, there is a list of options available here so that things can
be handled just as you would wish.

This covers the basics of using dBASE IV, but it is a very
complex program which has many more features than I can
describe here. It has a "Report" mode for example, which is
in some ways similar to the "Queries" mode, but is designed
more for finding groups of entries than for locating single pieces

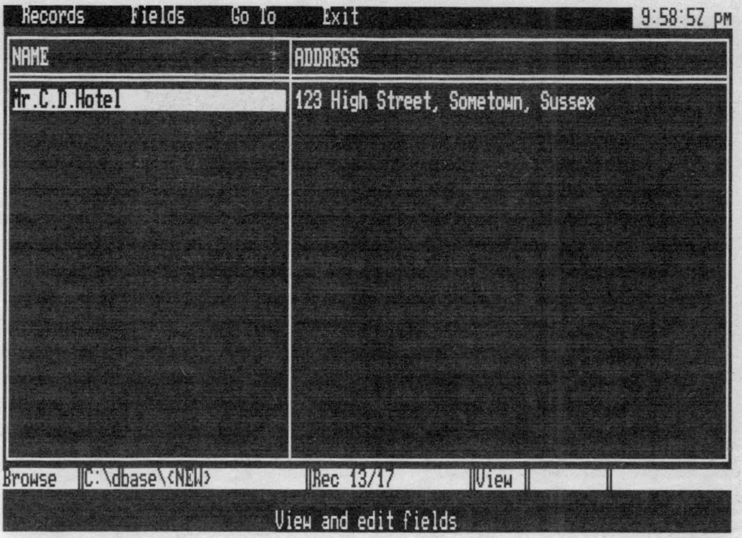
Records Fields Go To Exit
9:58:57 pm
NAME
ADDRESS
Mr.C.D.Hotel
123 High Street, Sometown, Sussex
Browse
C:\dbase\<NEW>
Rec 13/17
View
View and edit fields

Fig. 4.10 The example query of Figure 4.9 produces only a single match

of information. It is also possible to use dBASE IV as a sort of programming language, instead of the interactive mode described here. The information provided here should give you a good idea of the kinds of use to which a database program can be put, but if you wish to use a program of this type really effectively there is a fair amount to learn.

It is perhaps worth making the point that databases are not limited to simple database applications such as storing names, addresses, customer numbers, and the like. They are much used for things such as storing scientific data, such as the results obtained when testing new materials, products, or whatever. There are built-in mathematical functions which can be used to aid the assessment of the data, and some database programs can even produce graphs to further help with the analysis of data (but with many database programs a separate graphics program is needed for this type of thing). A good database such as dBASE IV is suitable for practically any database application,

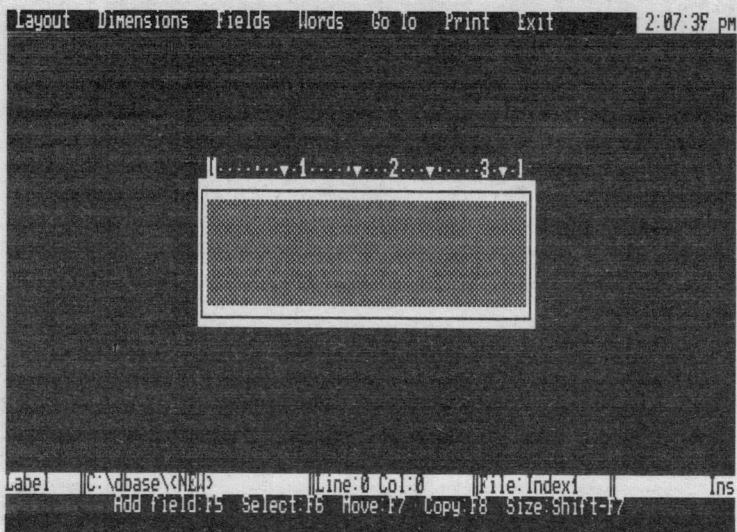

```
Label    ||C:\dbase\<NEW>        ||Line:0 Col:0    ||File:Index1 ||         Ins
         Add field:F5  Select:F6  Move:F7  Copy:F8  Size:Shift-F7
```

Fig. 4.11   The label design screen, complete with the default label in the centre of the screen

from simple name and address labelling through to complex scientific and technical applications.

Spreadsheets

The most popular spreadsheet program is Lotus 1-2-3, which at one time was the biggest selling computer program of all, and it possibly still is.   There are also several Lotus 1-2-3 "look-alikes", or "feel-alikes" as they are also known.   These are programs which are very much like the real thing in use, but which do not "borrow" any of the program coding from the original program. Two popular Lotus 1-2-3 look-alikes are "The Twin" and the renowned shareware program called "As Easy As".   The program used here in the spreadsheet examples is actually a version of "The Twin", but the information provided in this section on spreadsheets applies equally to any Lotus 1-2-3 style program.   In fact most of the information applies to any spreadsheet.

102

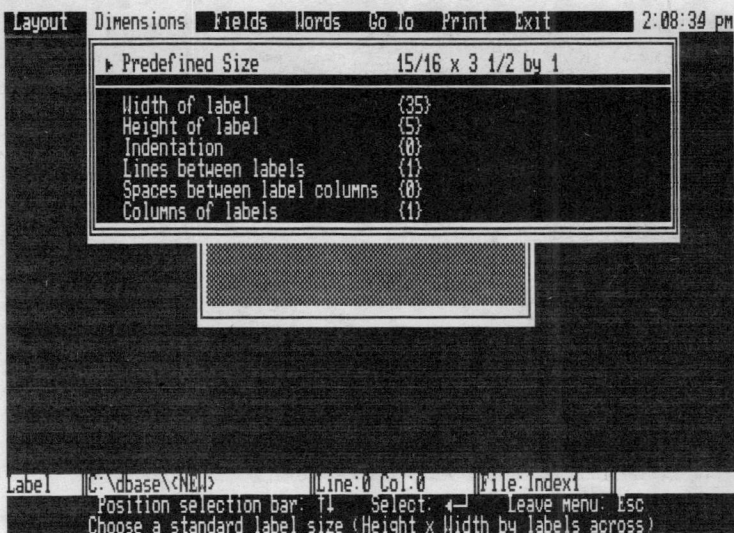

```
 Layout  Dimensions  Fields  Words  Go To  Print  Exit        2:08:34 pm
      ┌──────────────────────────────────────────────────────┐
      │ ▸ Predefined Size            15/16 x 3 1/2 by 1        │
      ├──────────────────────────────────────────────────────┤
      │   Width of label             {35}                      │
      │   Height of label            {5}                       │
      │   Indentation                {0}                       │
      │   Lines between labels       {1}                       │
      │   Spaces between label columns {0}                     │
      │   Columns of labels          {1}                       │
      └──────────────────────────────────────────────────────┘


 Label   C:\dbase\<NEW>          Line:0 Col:0       File:Index1
        Position selection bar: ↑↓    Select: ↵    Leave menu: Esc
        Choose a standard label size (Height x Width by labels across)
```

Fig. 4.12   A pop-down menu gives control over the size of the labels, etc.

As with databases, probably the best way of explaining what spreadsheets are all about is to dive straight in and look at how a practical program is used. We will not dwell at length on the subject of spreadsheets, since it is basically quite a simple idea. Once you understand the basic principle, either ideas for practical applications begin to flood into your mind, or they do not. Spreadsheets are well suited to those with a mathematical turn of mind, but are definitely not suited to those who shy away from figures.

The basic function of a spreadsheet is to provide mathematical calculations on the data entered into "cells". Figure 4.15 shows the initial screen, and the important part is the large upper section which contains the cells. The cells are identified using a sort of co-ordinate system. Each cell is identified by a letter and a number. To help you navigate your way around the spreadsheet the letters are shown across the top line of the screen, while the numbers are shown down the extreme left-hand side. Also, the currently selected cell is identified in the bottom

INDEX1	CALCULATED	PREDEFINED
ADDRESS	<create>	Date
COMPANY		Time
CUSTNUMBER		Recno
NAME		Pageno
POSTCODE		
TELNUMBER		

Label   C:\dbase\<NEW>   Opt 4/6   File:Index1
         Position selection bar: ↑↓   Select: ↵   Leave picklist: Esc

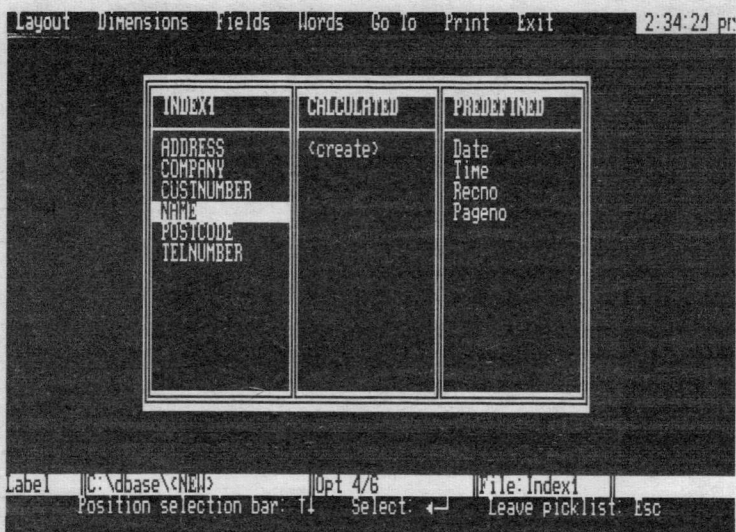

Fig. 4.13   Apart from user created fields, there are some predefined and (possibly) calculated fields available as well

left-hand corner of the screen. The top left-hand cell of the start-up screen is A-1, and the bottom right-hand cell is H-20. There are more cells than appear on the initial screen though, and the spreadsheet can be huge if necessary. The screen effectively acts as a "window" which enables the required part of the sheet to be viewed using a system of horizontal and vertical scrolling.

The function keys give access to some commands, as detailed on the penultimate line of the screen in Figure 4.15. The program is mainly controlled via a menuing system though. Pressing the backslash (" \ ") key produces the main menu on the third line up from the bottom of the screen, while the penultimate line shows the sub-menus available from the currently highlighted menu header word. This is shown in Figure 4.16. In many cases if you select a menu option, and then a sub-menu option, you may then be able to go even deeper into the menu system with sub-sub-menus. Like most modern high quality software, there are numerous features and facilities there if you want them.

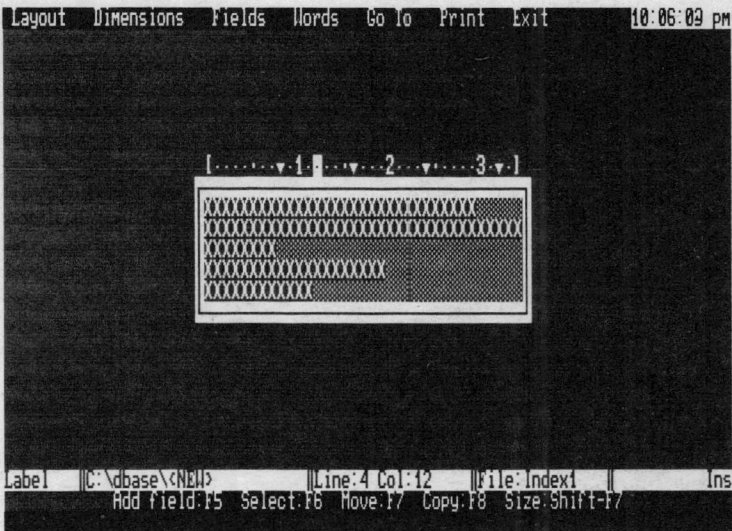

```
Layout  Dimensions  Fields  Words  Go To  Print  Exit          10:06:09 PM



              [·····ᵥ·1·█··ᵥ··2···ᵥ·····3·ᵥ·]

           ┌──────────────────────────────────────────┐
           │XXXXXXXXXXXXXXXXXXXXXXXXXXXXXXXXXXXXXXXXX   │
           │XXXXXXXXXXXXXXXXXXXXXXXXXXXXXXXXXXXXXXXXXX  │
           │XXXXXXXXX                                  │
           │XXXXXXXXXXXXXXXXXXXXXXXXXX                  │
           │XXXXXXXXXXXXX                              │
           └──────────────────────────────────────────┘




Label   C:\dbase\<NEW>           Line:4 Col:12    File:Index1           Ins
       Add field:F5  Select:F6  Move:F7  Copy:F8  Size:Shift-F7
```

*Fig. 4.14   The label design process has been completed, and a "dummy"
label is displayed*

Figure 4.17 shows a simple Twin demonstration spreadsheet
which shows the basic way in which the cells are used. Some of
the cells are simply used for labels which aid the user when
entering data into the program, or extracting information from
it. Particularly with complex spreadsheets, it is essential to make
extensive use of labels so that you know exactly what everything
is. Labels can be quite long if necessary, and they do not have to
fit into a standard size cell. Many of the cells contain figures that
are entered by the user, which in this case are prices in dollars.
Some of the other cells also contain values, but these are prices
that are calculated by the program from the data supplied by the
user. Rather than entering values into these cells, the user must
enter the correct formula. It is the value calculated from the
formula and the appropriate data that appears in the cell, and not
the formula itself. However, the left-hand section of the bottom
line of the screen shows the contents of the currently selected
cell, and where appropriate this shows a formula and not the value

105

Fig. 4.15   The initial spreadsheet screen. The main screen area contains the cells

contained by the cell in question. The selected cell is shown in inverse video in the upper part of the screen incidentally, and the cursor keys are used to select the required cell. In Figure 4.17 it is cell F-6 that has been selected. This cell contains a formula, and at the bottom of the screen it is therefore the formula that is shown, and not the calculated value. This enables you to check the formulae in use, and to add or edit them when necessary.

In this example the formula is "@SUM −F3 +F4". The "@" part tells the program that the cell contains a formula, and the "SUM" part of the formula is simply telling the computer to add together the contents of the specified cells. In this case they are cells F-3 and F-4, but there is a complication in that F-3 contains expenditure, not income. Therefore, a minus sign is used ahead of "F3" to make it a negative quantity, effectively making it a debit instead of a credit. Although in this example we are dealing with just two cells, a formula can be made to operate on any

106

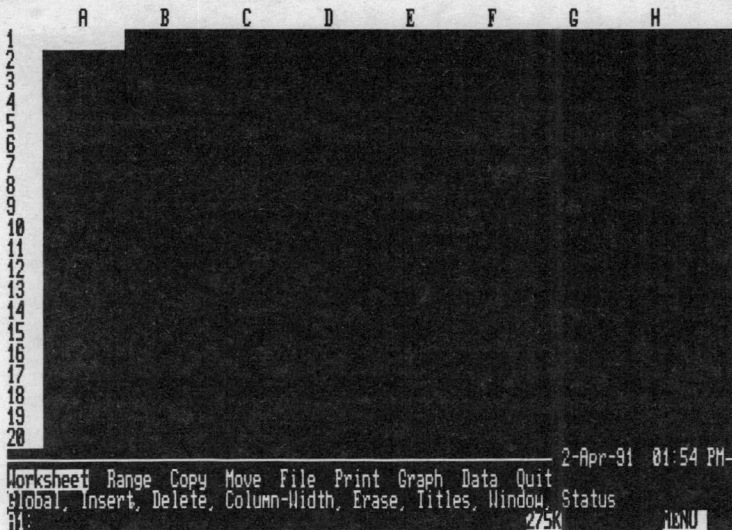

```
        A     B     C     D     E     F     G     H
1
2
3
4
5
6
7
8
9
10
11
12
13
14
15
16
17
18
19
20
                                           2-Apr-91  01:54 PM
Worksheet  Range  Copy  Move  File  Print  Graph  Data  Quit
Global, Insert, Delete, Column-Width, Erase, Titles, Window, Status
A1:                                        275K              MENU
```

Fig. 4.16 The menu system has been activated, and the main menu
appears near the bottom of the screen

number of cells.

If the spreadsheet must add up the prices of two hundred
items in a list, then it can easily be made to do this. You do not
have to include all two hundred cells in the formula individually,
and you can simply specify the range of cells to be processed
(D-1 to D-200 or whatever). Where necessary you can specify a
block of cells by giving the cells at diagonally opposite corners
(e.g. A-1 to C-25 would specify cells A-1 to A-25, B-1 to B25,
and C-1 to C-25). A range is specified by using two full stops
between the two delimiters (i.e. "A1..C25" in our example
range). Although we have only used a very simple formula in
this example, extremely complex formulae can be used if
necessary. Some specialised formulae are available as standard,
such as types for calculating interest. Others you must put
together yourself.

In most cases spreadsheets product calculation very rapidly,
but it is only fair to point out that with large amounts of data

107

	A	B	C	D	E	F
1		Q 1	Q 2	Q 3	Q 4	Total /83
2						
3	Total expense	$125,000	$119,000	$171,000	$128,000	$543,000
4	Total revenue	$245,000	$212,000	$168,500	$195,000	$820,500
5						
6	Profit/loss	$120,000	$93,000	($2,500)	$67,000	$277,500
7						
8						
9						
10		PICASSO	MONET	REMBRANT	CEZANNE	MICHAELANGELO
11						
12	HAWAII	55000	27000	29000	9600	33550
13	BAHAMAS	22500	29580	23000	3600	15670
14						
15		$77,500	$56,580	$52,000	$13,200	$49,220
16	Totals					248500
17						
18						
19						
20						

2-Apr-91 08:38 PM

F1-Help 2-Edit 3-Name 4-Abs 5-Goto 6-Window 7-Query 8-Table 9-Calc 10-Graph
F6: (C0) @SUM(-F3+F4)   269K   READY

Fig. 4.17   A demonstration setup which does some simple accounting

and highly complex formulae the results can be supplied something less than instantly. In fact you could be left waiting for
results for a considerable period of time in extreme cases. A fast
PC fitted with a maths co-processor is a good idea if you will do
a lot of work of this type.

All Change
The big attraction of spreadsheets for many users is their ability
to quickly respond to any changes that are made to either the
data or the formula in use. If a change is made then the program
will immediately recalculate any results that are affected, and
display the new results. This is not just useful for making speedy
corrections when mistakes are made. It is much used for so-
called "what if?" calculating. In other words, you first set everything up as you expect things to be, and look at the results.
You then explore your various options, altering the data and (or)
formulae, to suit various eventualities. It could be that there is a
better way of handling matters than the one your originally had

108

in mind. It could also be that there are sets of circumstances that you must avoid at all costs, or unforeseen circumstances that can be accommodated provided you plan for them properly.

This sort of financial modelling and planning is a major application of spreadsheets, and is probably the application that laid the foundation for their immense popularity. Spreadsheets are equally suitable for more simple accounting tasks, etc., or at the other extreme they are also suitable for many scientific and technical applications. In these scientific and technical roles spreadsheets can be used to mathematically model just about anything if they are fed with the right formulae, and their ability to rapidly recalculate everything when modifications are made is more than a little useful when undertaking this type of thing.

It is only fair to point out that spreadsheets are no longer the automatic choice for some mathematical applications. For accounting and financial planning there are now specialised programs for these tasks. These range from simple accounting programs for one-man cash only businesses, through to suites of financial programs that can handle just about everything financial, even for quite large businesses. There are also programs designed specifically for scientific calculations and graphing. A spreadsheet has the versatility to handle just about any type of mathematical application, but it could take some time to get it set up to operate properly in your particular applications. Specialist mathematical programs are likely to be easier to set up and use, and might be somewhat superior, but will almost certainly be quite costly if you need to buy several of these programs to cover a range of specialist tasks.

It is perhaps worth mentioning that spreadsheet programs usually have quite good graphics capabilities. They have what is effectively a built-in business graphics program, which usually has the ability to handle a certain amount of technical graphing. There are the usual options which enable the X and Y axis ranges to be specified, labels to be specified, etc. There are also some less common ones, such as the choice of logarithmic or linear scaling on each axis, which is useful for some scientific graphing.

The graphs are based on data from specified cell ranges, and in most cases one of these ranges would contain data calculated by the program. Things do not have to be done this way though,

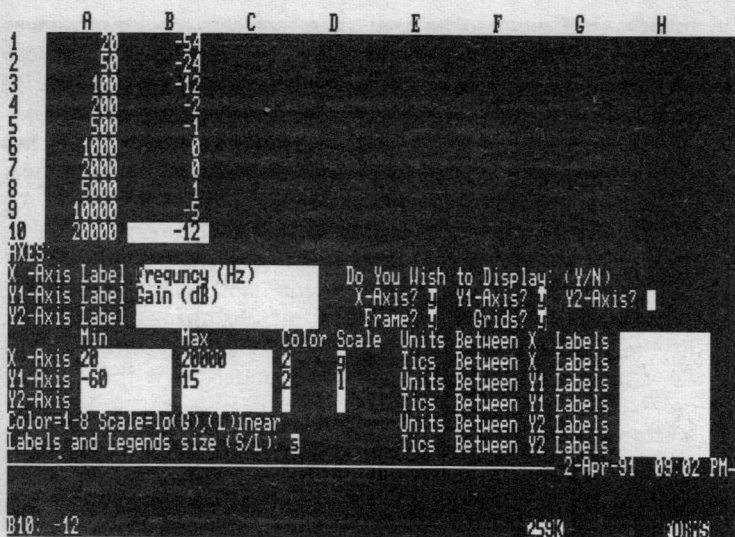

Fig. 4.18   A "Graph" sub-menu, together with same sample data

and the graphs can be produced directly from data supplied by the user. When used in this way the program is really operating as a straightforward graphics program rather than a spreadsheet. Figure 4.18 shows one of the "Graph" sub-menus, together with some data in the upper section of the screen. Figure 4.19 shows the line graph produced from this data.

When dealing with spreadsheets you are likely to encounter references to "3-D spreadsheets". These are much the same as ordinary spreadsheets in essence, but you effectively have a number of spreadsheets piled one on top of the other. Obviously you can only view one layer at a time on the two-dimensional monitor screen. Cells have the usual identification letter and number, plus an additional number which indicates how many layers down into the spreadsheet the cell appears.

Although it might seem that a 3-D spreadsheet is not much different to a two dimensional type for which a number of sheets have been created and stored away on disk, this is not really the case. Remember that with a number of separate sheets

110

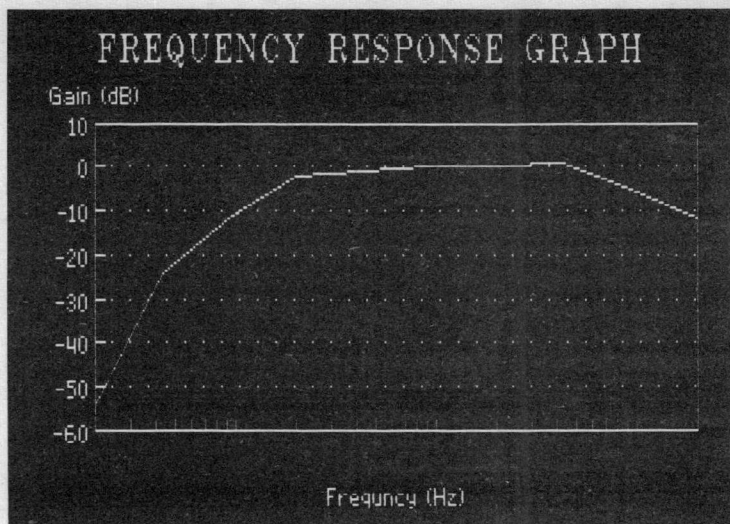

Fig. 4.19   The line graph produced from the data of Figure 4.18. Note the logarithmic scaling of the X axis

it is difficult to make calculations based on more than one sheet. In fact you might have to merge all the sheets into one long (and probably confusing) "mega" sheet in order to do this properly. For some applications a 3-D spreadsheet enables the data to be organised more logically, and calculations based on any group of cells can be handled with ease. Things can still be a bit confusing even with the aid of a 3-D spreadsheet though, and advanced 3-D mathematical modelling is perhaps best left to those with advanced 3-D mathematical minds!

Integration
Most computer users probably buy individual pieces of software to suit their requirements, but there is an alternative in the form of integrated software. These are sets of (usually) three or four programs which include a word processor, a database, a spreadsheet, and a business graphics program. In some cases they are programs that are run completely separately, while in other cases

111

you have what seems to be one huge program, but what in truth is probably several separate programs with a control program that permits rapid switching from one to the other.

Integrated software has definite attractions, one of which is competitive pricing. Buying comparable software in the form of separate programs would probably cost much more than buying an integrated suite. Another advantage is that with integrated software it is usually quite straightforward if you wish to swap data between programs.

Despite these potential advantages integrated suites do not seem to have sold as well as individual word processors, spreadsheet programs, etc. One reason for this is that the programs in most integrated suites do not have facilities to rival the best individual pieces of software. In some cases the capabilities of the programs in an integrated suite are decidedly limited. Even where the programs have good specifications, some programs in the set will probably meet your requirements better than others. By buying individual programs you can select each one to closely match your needs without having to make any major compromises.

Utilities

One general type of software that is definitely worthy of inclusion here is the utility type. Programs of this type provide aid with the management of disk files in particular, but also the computer in general. In addition to a substantial amount of normal commercial software of this type, utilities are also to be found in abundance in shareware catalogues. These usually list numerous disks which contain compilations of simple utility programs, plus a few that contain more major utility software. The commercial utility software is mainly of the "all singing — all dancing" variety, and there are some really excellent commercial programs of this type such as PC Tools and the Norton Utilities.

Every PC is equipped with an operating system (MS/DOS or an equivalent) which provides numerous facilities for handling the day-to-day running of the computer. So why do you need the extra facilities offered by these utility programs? Although you get a number of useful utilities as part of the computer's operating system, I (and many others) have nevertheless come to regard some good additional utility software as an essential part of computing with a PC. The reason for this is simply that the operating system provides the basic facilities that you will need, but there are some useful extras which make computing life so much easier. Also, there are some facilities offered by the operating system which are adequate, but which can be improved upon.

As a simple example, what happens if you accidentally erase a disk file? The facilities offered by the operating system do not include any way of restoring a "zapped" file, but a program such as PC Tools will usually enable such a file to be recovered, provided none of it has been overwritten by a subsequent file. Although file recovery of this type may seem to be completely impossible, it is not actually that difficult. You need to bear in mind that when a file is deleted, it is not actually wiped from the disk, and is actually left intact. The disk contains a directory which includes the names of the files on the disk, and where each one is situated. When a file is deleted, the directory is altered to indicate that the file is no longer there, but the file itself is left unaltered.

When you enter the PC Tools "disk services" you obtain the screen shown in Figure 4.20. It is only fair to point out that the screen dumps provided here were produced using what is not the most recent version of PC Tools, but this version is fairly typical of general utility software, and it nicely demonstrates the sorts of facility that are available from this type of program. To undelete a file you press the "U" key, and then direct the program to the appropriate disk, etc., where the file can be found. The program then scans the disk and reports any deleted files that it has located (Fig. 4.21).

The first character of each file is given as a question mark (?), simply because this character is erased from the disk when a file is erased. In some cases automatic file recovery is possible, and then all you have to do is supply the missing character in the file name, using any valid character if you do not know the right one (which you presumably would in most cases).

Automatic recovery of some files is not possible, and some manual editing of the data on the disk is then required in order to recover the file. This is dependent on you having suitable technical knowledge and knowledge of the deleted file. This might mean that in practice the file can not be recovered.

113

PC Tools Deluxe R4.22
Disk and Special Functions
DISK SERVICES: Copy cOmpare Find Rename Verify view/Edit Map Locate iNitialize
SPECIAL SERVICES: Directory maint Undelete system Info Park Help
F3=file srvc F10=F3+chg drv Esc=exit PC Tools

Fig. 4.20 The initial PC Tools screen. The disk services available are listed at the bottom of the screen

Problems are most likely to occur where part of the file has been overwritten, which obviously means that it can not be fully recovered. There can also be problems with fragmented files. This is where the file is not on the disk in one place, but is spread across it in several small blocks of data. In most cases though, provided you have not written anything to the disk since deleting the file, it can be recovered without difficulty. Also, if you should happen to accidentally wipe out a number of files, it will probably be possible to recover them all.

Utility programs usually offer a range of other facilities. At the most basic level there are simple commands, such as ones to permit the renaming of a directory or sub-directory, or to give some basic information about the computer. Figure 4.22 for instance, shows the PC Tools report on the hardware and performance of my Dell System 200 PC. I would caution against believing everything that a report program tells you. I have rarely found them to get everything right. In this case it has reported

PC Tools Deluxe R4.22   Vol Label=None
                          Undelete Services   Scroll Lock OFF
Path=C:*.*

Name	Ext	Size	Attr	Date	Name	Ext	Size	Attr	Date
?CAD10	COM	3343	...A	4/20/91	?ILE0011	CHK@	4096	....	3/10/91
?ILE0001	CHK@	32768	....	3/10/91	?ILE0018	CHK	2048	....	12/16/90
?ILE0002	CHK@	2048	....	3/10/91	?ILE0019	CHK	2048	....	12/16/90
?ASS	EXE	46021	...A	10/27/89	?ILE0020	CHK	61440	....	12/16/90
?SQUARE	BAT@	293	...A	12/21/90	?ILE0021	CHK	61440	....	12/16/90
?ILE0003	CHK@	2048	....	3/10/91	?ILE0022	CHK	2048	....	12/16/90
?ILE0004	CHK@	2048	....	3/10/91	?ILE0023	CHK	2048	....	12/16/90
?ILE0005	CHK@	2048	....	3/10/91	?ILE0024	CHK	2048	....	12/16/90
?ILE0006	CHK@	2048	....	3/10/91	?ILE0025	CHK	2048	....	12/16/90
?ILE0007	CHK@	12288	....	3/10/91	?ILE0026	CHK	12288	....	12/16/90
?ILE0008	CHK@	83968	....	3/10/91	?ILE0027	CHK	12288	....	12/16/90
?ILE0009	CHK@	20480	....	3/10/91	?ILE0028	CHK	2048	....	12/16/90
?ILE0010	CHK@	65536	....	3/10/91	?ILE0029	CHK	49152	....	12/16/90

```
                    @ = Automatic recovery possible
        Select file(s) to be un-deleted and then press "@" to proceed.
   F8=directory LIST argument  F9=file SELECTion argument  F10=chg drive/path
      ▲▼=scroll  ←=SELECT  ↑=UNselect  F2=alt dir lst  Esc=exit
```

Fig. 4.21   A long list of deleted files for recovery. Automatic recovery is
only possible on some of these

the presence of a logical drive E which is not there, and has
missed some 512K of extended memory.

Other typical features include disk maps. This is a diagram
which shows how the disk space is utilized, as in the example of
Figure 4.23. A directory tree is another common feature. This
shows the directories and sub-directories of a disk. In the case
of floppy disks directories and sub-directories are often not used,
as the disk capacities are so small as to make them unnecessary
in most cases. However, hard disks usually have quite complex
directory arrangements, and a directory tree gives a simple
graphical representation of how things are organised. Figure 4.24
shows part of a directory tree. Vertical scrolling enables the off-
screen part of the tree to be examined.

If you are not familiar with directories, it should perhaps be
explained that these are simply a means of notionally compart-
mentalising a disk. You start off in the root directory of a disk,
and the directories branch out from this. The basic idea is to

```
PC Tools Deluxe R4.22
---------------------------System Information Service---------------------------

                                    Computer - IBM/PC AT
                     The BIOS programs are dated - 01/15/88
                                Operating system - DOS 3.30
                  Number of logical disk drives - 5
                     Logical drive letter range - A thru E
                                   Serial Ports - 2
                                 Parallel Ports - 1
                                       CPU Type - 80286
                Relative speed (orig PC=100%) - 590%
                    Math co-processor present - 80287
     User programs are loaded at HEX paragraph - 2096
       Memory used by DOS and resident programs - 133472 bytes
            Memory available for user programs - 521888 bytes
                    Total memory reported by DOS - 640K
     PC Tools has found the total memory to be - 640K
     Enhanced Graphics Adapter present (color) - 256K
                           Expanded memory total - 2048K, in use - 0K
    Additional ROM BIOS found at HEX paragraph - C000K


Press any key to return
```

Fig. 4.22 The report on the hardware, etc., of my AT computer, which includes some errors

have each program in its own directory, with perhaps data for that program in separate directories. These can either branch out from the program's directory, or from the root directory, as preferred. You can go on making sub-directories of sub-directories indefinitely if you wish, but doing this type of thing to excess can cause more problems than it solves.

A hard disk often contains around one to two thousand files, and having all these in a single directory would not be very convenient. Sensible use of directories and sub-directories keeps things much more manageable. For example, if you wish to remove a program complete with its support files and data files, this is easily achieved if these are kept separate from everything else in one or two sub-directories. The operating system provides commands that enable all the files in a directory to be deleted en-masse. If the files are mixed in with hundreds of others, they will have to be deleted one by one. In the example directory tree there is a directory called "DOS" which contains the operating

```
                    ▓ Available    File Alloc Table  . Allocated ▓ Read Only
                    ▓ Boot record  ▒ Directory        ▒ hidden   ▓ Bad Cluster
Entire disk mapped                                              9% free space
.................................................................▓...▓....▓.
.................................................................
...........................................................▓..▒.▓.
...........................................................▓.▒.▓
...........................................................▒.▓.▓
...........................................................▓.▓.▓
...........................................................▓.▓.▒
.................................⊠.........................▒.▓.▒.▓..
...........................................................▓.▓.▒.▓.
...........................................................▓.▓
.................................................................▒
```

Each position is equivalent to 1/1000th of the total space. (left to right)

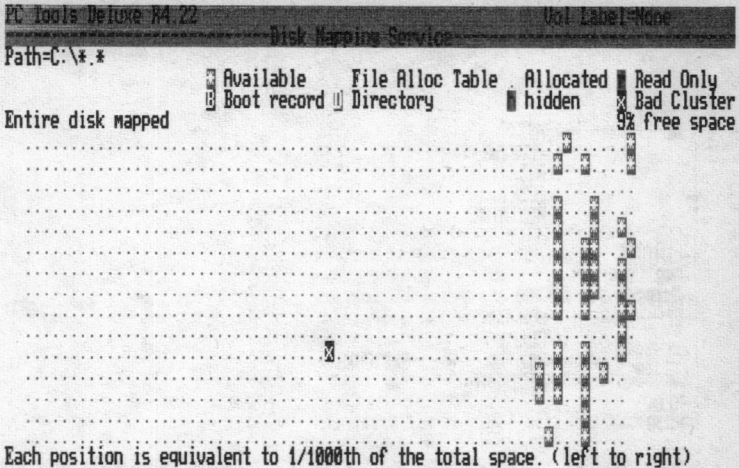

```
       ▓ "F" to map files. ESC to return ▓
```

*Fig. 4.23   A disk map which shows how the available storage space of a
hard disk is utilized*

system files, one called "MONEY" which contains an accounting
program, and one called "WP" which contains the Wordperfect
word processor program used to produce this book. The sub-
directories from the "WP" directory each contain a book manuscript ("PCSFTBK") being the one for the manuscript of this
book). With the aid of a directory tree you can see at a glance
how the directories and sub-directories of a disk are organised.

It is only possible to cover a few typical utility applications
here — there must be hundreds of different functions available
from countless utility programs. It is well worth arming yourself
with a selection of utility software which should make the day-
to-day running of the computer system much easier, and can
"save the day" if things should go wrong. Perhaps that should be
when rather than if things go wrong.

WIMPS

By their very nature, computers are highly technical items. This

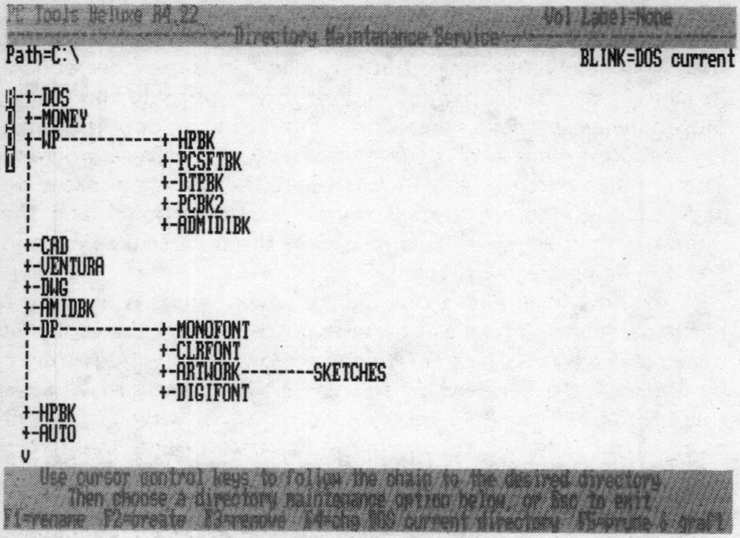

Path=C:\   BLINK=DOS current

```
+-+-DOS
  +-MONEY
  +-WP-----------+-HPBK
  |              +-PCSFTBK
  |              +-DTPBK
  |              +-PCBK2
  |              +-ADMIDIBK
  +-CAD
  +-VENTURA
  +-DWG
  +-AMIDBK
  +-DP-----------+-MONOFONT
  |              +-CLRFONT
  |              +-ARTWORK--------SKETCHES
  |              +-DIGIFONT
  +-HPBK
  +-AUTO
v
```

Use cursor control keys to follow the chain to the desired directory
then choose a directory maintenance option below, or Esc to exit.
F1=rename F2=create F3=remove F4=chg the current directory F5=prune & graft

Fig. 4.24   A directory tree enables you to see at a glance how the sub-
directories of a disk are organised

has tended to put many people off the idea of using computers,
and made life difficult for non-technically minded people who
decided to try their hand at computing. WIMPs (windows —
icons — mouse — pointer) are programs that are designed to make
computing more accessible, making it relatively easy for non-
technical people to use computers. With an ordinary operating
system you have to type in commands such as "del homework.
asc" in order to undertake simple tasks such as deleting files,
formatting disks ready for use, etc. In order to do this you have
to know the command words. Perhaps of greater significance,
you also need to know the right syntax. A space or a comma out
of place and the computer will almost certainly refuse to carry
out the command. Worse still, you might accidentally tell it to
do the wrong thing.

WIMPs have a totally different approach using a graphical user
interface (GUI). In other words, on the screen there are pictures
to represent programs, disk drives, or whatever. These are the

icons. The mouse controls an on-screen pointer which is used to select the desired icon by placing the pointer on the icon and then "clicking" the mouse button once. In some cases double "clicking" is required, which simply means pressing the mouse button twice in rapid succession. For example, double "clicking" on a program icon is the normal way of running a program. There is also "dragging", which is where the pointer is placed on an icon, the mouse button is pressed and held down, and the mouse is then moved. This results in the pointer moving, and the icon being dragged along with it.

A window is simply a box on the screen which is used for a particular task. There can be several windows on the screen at once, each with its own specific function. One window might be showing the contents of another disk, and a third window running an accessory program such as an on-screen clock or calculator. The windows can be dragged around the screen using the mouse and positioned where you want them. In most cases they can also be altered in size and shape.

Probably the two most popular WIMP programs are Windows and GEM. Figure 4.25 shows a Windows screen dump. This black and white illustration can not really do justice to a Windows

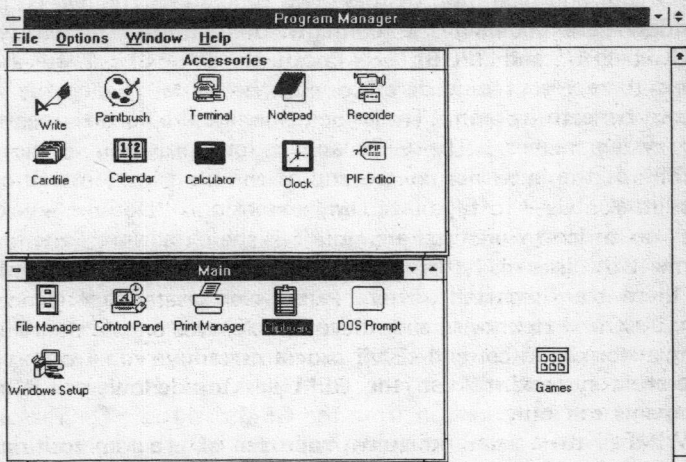

Fig. 4.25   A Windows screen dump showing two windows

screen, as these are almost invariably very colourful. There are two windows open in this example, stacked one above the other on the left-hand section of the screen. The lower window ("Main") is active, as the name at the top of the screen is in inverse video, and the controls are visible at the ends of this header line. The control box at the left-hand end of the header line is used to bring down the system menu. The two controls at the other end of the header line are the minimise and maximise controls. These respectively reduce the window to an icon, and expand it to fill the available screen area. To make a window active you simply "click" the mouse on it.

There are two basic types of window, which are document windows and program windows. In this example the windows are both document types, and these show icons for applications programs, data files, facilities available from windows, and this type of thing. A program window is different in that it normally includes a menu bar, and it obviously contains a running application of some kind. The Corel Draw! screen dumps in Chapter 2 show program windows.

Figure 4.26 shows a GEM 3 start-up screen. In GEM terminology this is the GEM desktop. This has similarities to the Windows 3 example screen, but there are marked differences in the layout and operation of these two programs. The two GEM windows are showing the contents of two disk directories ("GEMAPPS" and "PUBLISH", both on drive C). There are icons to represent each disk file, and the name of each file is shown beneath its icon. These file names are the normal operating system names. The GEM applications programs all have "APP" as the extension at the end of the file name, instead of the usual DOS "EXE" or "COM" extensions. Double "clicking" on an icon which has an "APP" as the extension in the file name will "launch" this application (i.e. run the program).

There is an important difference between programs that have .EXE/.COM extensions, and those which have an .APP extension. Normal .COM and .EXE programs can be run from the operating system or from the GEM desktop. However, .APP programs can only be run from the GEM desktop. The reason for this is that these programs make use of program routines provided by GEM, and can only function properly if these routines have first been loaded into the computer's memory.

120

```
┌─────────────────────────────────────────────────────────────┐
│ ▸│                    C:\GEMAPPS\                           ▸ │
├─────────────────────────────────────────────────────────────┤
│                                                               │
│   📁        📁        📁        📁        💻                  │
│  New Folder  CLIPBRD   FONTS    GEMSYS   OUTPUT.APP  OUTPUT.INF  OUTPUT.RSC │
│                                                               │
└─────────────────────────────────────────────────────────────┘
┌─────────────────────────────────────────────────────────────┐
│ ▸│                    C:\PUBLISH\                           ▸ │
├─────────────────────────────────────────────────────────────┤
│   📁        📁        📁        📁                            │
│  New Folder   DTP     PICTURES  STORIES    CHS    FONTWID.APP  PUBLISH.APP │
│                                                               │
│  CHSDTP.DTP  FRAME.DTP  TEST.DTP  UNTITLED.DTP  PUB_DOCS.HLP  PUB_DRAW.HLP  PUB_FRAM.HLP │
│                                                               │
│  PUB_KYBD.HLP  PUB_PAGE.HLP  PUB_PARA.HLP  PUB_PICT.HLP  PUB_STYL.HLP  PUB_TEXT.HLP  PUBLISH.HVP │
│                                                               │
│  PUB_ES.OVL  PUB_FR.OVL  PUB_IE.OVL  PUB_IG.OVL  PUB_IT.OVL  PUB_TX.OVL  FONTWID.RSC │
└─────────────────────────────────────────────────────────────┘
```

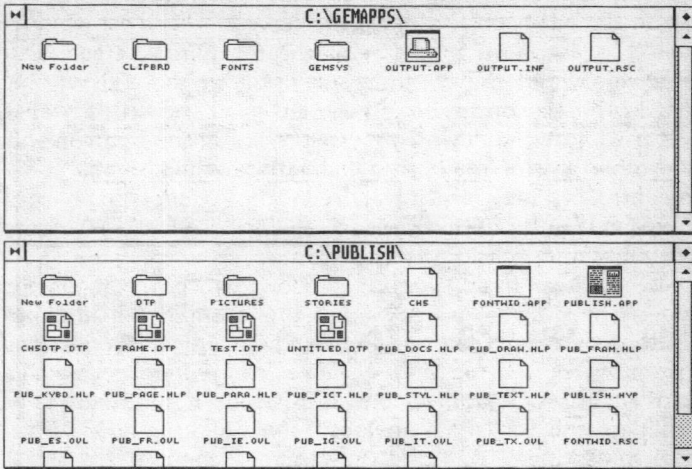

Fig. 4.26   A GEM 3 start up screen with two windows

The Timeworks DTP program is an example of a GEM based
program of this type, and it is actually supplied complete with
the full GEM 3 program. This is unusual, and most GEM programs are either not supplied with GEM at all, or come complete
with a run-time version. This is a sort of bare-bones version of
GEM which is loaded automatically before the main program is
run, and provides the facilities that the program requires, but
nothing more. With this system you can not run GEM on its
own, as the full desktop program is not present. The Ventura
DTP program is one which is supplied complete with a run time
version of GEM.

Note that there is a similar situation with Windows. Normal
MS/DOS software can be run from Windows, but there are programs which can only be run from Windows. Some of these
programs are supplied with a run time version of Windows, but
others require the full Windows program to be purchased separately. Corel Draw! is an example of a Windows application that is
not supplied with a run time version of Windows. It is also worth

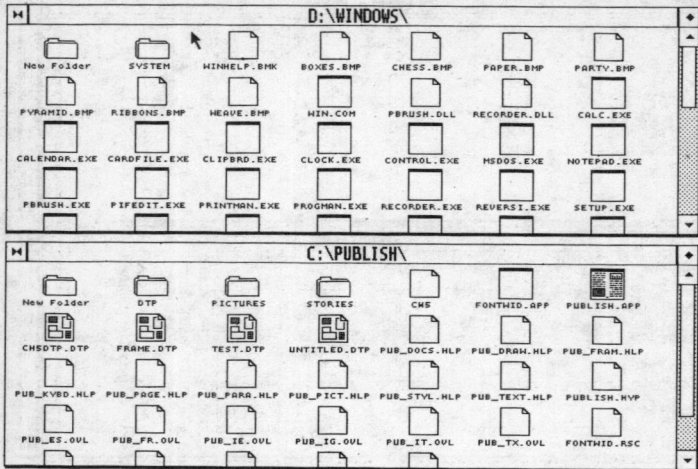

Fig. 4.27   With a large number of files the scroll bar becomes smaller

noting that some programs will only operate with a particular version or versions of GEM or Windows. Programs intended for use with Windows version 3 for instance, will not work with earlier versions such as Windows version 2.

You will notice in Figure 4.26 that the lower window is not large enough to display all the icons for the "Publish" directory, and that some icons are chopped off at the bottom of the screen. You will also notice a control down the right-hand side of the window. This is called a scroll bar, and it can be manipulated using the mouse to scroll the window so that the icons at the bottom of the window are brought into view. This is a vertical scroll bar, but a horizontal type can be used instead of or in addition to a vertical scroll bar.

With a small window and (or) a lot of icons to be displayed, the scroll bar becomes quite small. In the upper window of Figure 4.27 for instance, the scroll bar is only about one-third of the window's height. Dragging the scroll bar down to the bottom of its slide range therefore results in all the original icons being

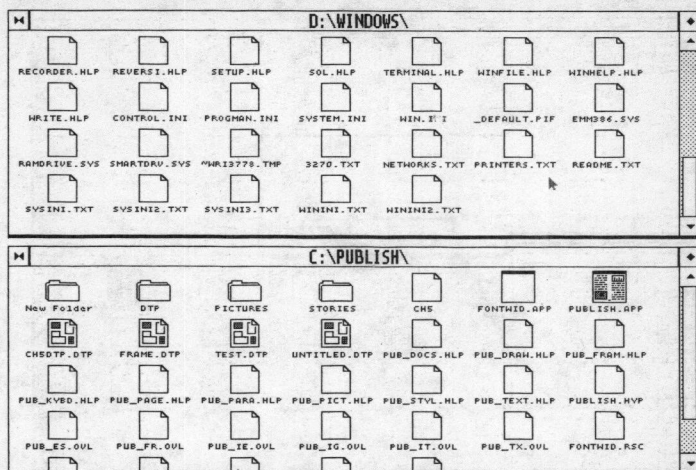

Fig. 4.28   The upper scroll bar has been moved down to bring a different set of file icons into the top window

scrolled off the top of the window, and a completely new set appearing (Fig. 4.28). Taking the scroll bar to the middle of its slide range would reveal yet more icons. In an extreme case there could be a dozen or more windows-full of icons, and a lot of scrolling could be needed in order to find the icon you require. GEM can provide a list of file names instead of sets of icons, and where large numbers of files are involved the list of names is probably the more manageable option.

You will notice an icon in the top left-hand corner of the upper window marked "new folder". In GEM terminology there is no such thing as a directory or sub-directory, and all files are placed in folders. Folders and directories are just different terms for the same thing though. Double "clicking" on the new folder icon brings up a dialogue box (Fig. 4.29). The name of the new folder is typed in via the keyboard, which is still needed in a WIMP environment, and then the "OK" box is "clicked" in order to produce the new folder/directory. You simply "click" on the "Cancel" box if you change your mind.

123

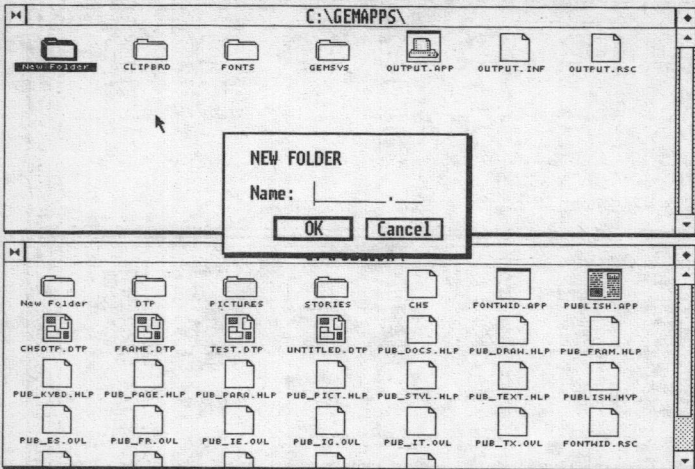

Fig. 4.29   Double "clicking" on the "New Folder" icon brings up a dialogue box

In order to go into a folder and display its contents you simply double "click" on its icon. The contents of the window then change to display the files present in the folder. In order to go back up the directory tree again you simply "click" on the control box in the top left-hand corner of the window. If you "click" on this enough times you will eventually obtain the disk drive icons, as in Figure 4.30. You can then click on the icon for a different drive, and this enables you to switch to a different drive.

In order to copy a file from one folder to another, you simply display the contents of both folders on the screen, and then drag the file from one folder to the other. In order to delete a file you simply "click" on it once, and then select the delete option from the "File" drop-down menu. A dialogue gives you the opportunity to change your mind or go ahead with the deletion. Once you have the basic idea it is not difficult to control the computer using a GUI. If you do not know how something is achieved, a little experimentation will usually bring results. For

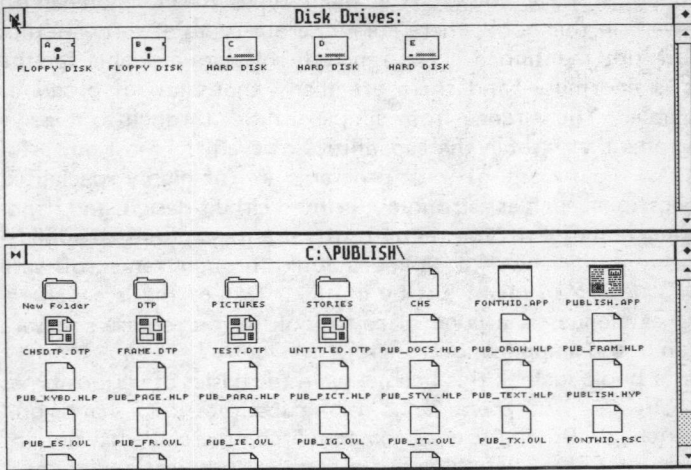

Fig. 4.30   Moving up the directory tree to the disk drive icons (top window)

non-technical people they can certainly make computing very much easier. In due course many people seem to outgrow them, but in the mean time they provide a relatively "painless" intro-duction to computing.

It is perhaps worth mentioning menuing programs. These are normally set to run automatically at switch-on, and are set up so that you can run the desired program, or exit into the operating system, simply by selecting the appropriate menu option and pressing the "Return" key. The ideal is for someone who has a reasonable knowledge of computers to set things up so that even the most non-technical of people can run the required program. This type of software is much used in companies where com-puters are used by non-computer literate personnel, and usually seem to be very successful. However, with an arrangement of this type you really need someone with a knowledge of comput-ing to oversee things and sort out the inevitable problems (e.g. "What do I do now the hard disk is full?").

Finally

Although I have covered the main types of PC (non-games) software in this book, there are numerous types of software that I have not mentioned. The range of software available for the PCs is enormous, and there are many thousands of programs available. These range from simple utilities through to massive programs that stretch the capabilities of even the most powerful PCs. A great many of these programs are for highly specialised applications, such as astronomy, printed circuit design, and handwriting analysis. If you require software for an unusual application, then it is worth taking a look through some software catalogues. You might just be in luck. One of the larger shareware catalogues is a good place to look if you require software for an unusual application.

In a book such as this I can explain the basics of various types of software, but there is no real substitute for "hands-on" experience. Buying lots of expensive commercial software for use as a training exercise is not a practical proposition for most of us. Demonstration versions of many commercial programs are available free or at very low cost, and a fair percentage of these can provide you with a lot of valuable practical experience. The least useful demonstration software is the type which provides a running demonstration where you just sit and watch while it goes through its "party pieces". There are interactive demonstrations which are of a little more value. With these you have what is basically a running demonstration, but you have to operate the right keys at the right times as you go through some simple tutorial sessions.

The demonstration programs that are of most use are the ones which are almost fully operational and useable versions of the real thing. The program is disabled in some way, which in most cases means that there is no way of saving work to disk, and it might not be possible to print anything out either. This means that the program can not be used in earnest, but you can spend a long time trying out its various functions, and learning a great deal about that particular type of software. Some demonstration programs are fully operational in every way, but will only run a few times and then become unusable. In a similar vein, some programs are fully operational but switch-off after they have been running for a certain period of time. In both cases this clearly enables you to fully try out and assess the software, again learning a great deal about that particular type of software in the process.

It is well worthwhile obtaining a selection of demonstration programs. It will enable you to determine with a fair degree of certainty the types of software that will be of real use to you. It should also make it clear which particular features are important to you, and which ones are of little or no practical value to you. You may well find that one or two of the programs you try out are just perfect for your requirements. As well as demonstration programs, do not overlook the mass of shareware software that is available. This also provides a means of trying out various programs of different types at low cost. If you should find something that is of real use to you, it does not usually cost a great deal to register your copy and become a legitimate user.

Probably the most important thing is not to dive straight in and spend large sums of money on software without looking at a range of alternative programs first. Ideally you should try out software before buying it. Although the specifications of software of a given type are often very similar, and they may look very similar in operation, they can actually be very different to use. An often overlooked aspect of computing is that you must find software intuitive in use if you are to use it efficiently. The only way to determine whether or not you get on well using a particular piece of software is to try it out, preferably for at least a few hours or more.

Index

Notes

132

Notes

Notes